Response to Intervention (RTI) and English Learners

Making It Happen

Jana Echevarría
California State University, Long Beach

MaryEllen Vogt
California State University, Long Beach

Boston   Columbus   Indianapolis   New York   San Francisco   Upper Saddle River
Amsterdam   Cape Town   Dubai   London   Madrid   Milan   Munich   Paris   Montreal
Toronto   Delhi   Mexico City   Sao Paulo   Sydney   Hong Kong   Seoul   Singapore   Taipei   Tokyo

Vice President, Editor-in-Chief: Aurora Martínez Ramos
Editorial Assistant: Meagan French
Marketing Manager: Danae April
Production Editor: Gregory Erb
Editorial Production Service: Nesbitt Graphics
Manufacturing Buyer: Megan Cochran
Electronic Composition: Nesbitt Graphics, Inc.
Interior Design: Nesbitt Graphics, Inc.
Photo Researcher: Annie Pickert
Cover Designer: Linda Knowles

For Professional Development resources visit www.pearsonpd.com.

Credits and acknowledgments borrowed from other sources and reproduced, with permission, in this textbook appear on appropriate page within text. Chapter opening photo credits: pp. 1, 61, 113, Bob Daemmrich Photography; p. 23, Lindfors Photography; p. 39, iStockphoto; p. 81, Ellen Senisi/The Image Works; p. 99, Bob Daemmrich/The Image Works.

Library of Congress Cataloging-in-Publication Data

Echevarria, Jana
  RTI and English learners : making it happen / Jana Echevarría, MaryEllen
Vogt.
     p. cm.
  Includes bibliographical references and index.
   ISBN 0-13-704890-4 (alk. paper)
 1. English language--Study and teaching--United States--Foreign speakers.
2. Language arts--Remedial teaching--United States. I. Vogt, MaryEllen.
II. Title.
 PE1128.A2E25 2011
 428.2'4--dc22
                             2010023179

10 9 8 7 6 5 4 3 2   BRG 14 13 12 11 10

www.pearsonhighered.com

ISBN-10: 0-13-704890-4
ISBN-13: 978-0-13-704890-8

Jana Echevarría is a Professor Emerita at California State University, Long Beach. She has taught in elementary, middle, and high schools in general education, special education, ESL, and bilingual programs. She has lived in Taiwan, Spain, and Mexico. An internationally known expert on second language learners, Dr. Echevarría is a Fulbright Specialist. Her research and publications focus on effective instruction for English learners, including those with learning disabilities. Currently, she is Co-Principal Investigator with the Center for Research on the Educational Achievement and Teaching of English Language Learners (CREATE) funded by the U.S. Department of Education, Institute of Education Sciences (IES). In 2005, Dr. Echevarría was selected as Outstanding Professor at CSULB.

MaryEllen Vogt is Professor Emerita of Education at California State University, Long Beach. Dr. Vogt has been a classroom teacher, reading specialist, special education specialist, curriculum coordinator, and university teacher educator. She received her doctorate from the University of California, Berkeley, and is a co-author of fifteen books, including *Reading Specialists and Literacy Coaches in the Real World* (3rd ed., 2011) and the SIOP® book series. Her research interests include improving comprehension in the content areas, teacher change and development, and content literacy and language acquisition for English learners. Dr. Vogt was inducted into the California Reading Hall of Fame, received her university's Distinguished Faculty Teaching Award, and served as President of the International Reading Association in 2004–2005.

contents

For many years, it wasn't unusual for a classroom teacher to approach special educators in the faculty room or school yard and tell them about a student who was struggling. The teacher suspected a problem and wanted to refer the student for special education services. This teacher completed a referral form and after parents were notified and agreed, the student was tested to see if there was an identifiable learning disability, which would be discerned by a significant discrepancy between the student's academic achievement scores (determined by standardized achievement tests) and IQ score (determined by a standardized intelligence test). Based on the results, and if warranted, the student was scheduled into special education classes, either for part of the day or for the entire day, depending on the nature of the identified disability. The special education teacher wrote an Individual Education Plan (IEP) that was reviewed at an IEP meeting attended by the special education and classroom teachers, an administrator, and the student's parents, and subsequent educational decisions were made based upon a once-a-year conference during an IEP meeting.

Seldom did any students exit special education.

Time went by and schools began forming student study teams (or something with a similar name and purpose) to discuss particular students' difficulties and recommend interventions before considering referral for special education assessment. Gradually, educators began to question why it was necessary for a student to fail or at least experience serious academic difficulties before help was given. Student study teams served as a pre-referral measure and had a preventive goal, so that students had a chance of overcoming academic weaknesses before special education eligibility was considered. This process was a marked improvement over the refer-test-identify-place approach of the past.

As a bilingual special education teacher (Echevarría) and a reading specialist/special education teacher (Vogt), we both experienced the serious disconnect between what we were teaching, how students performed academically in our classrooms, what was being taught in mainstream classrooms, and how these same students functioned in those classrooms. The process for assisting struggling learners (in special education and in general education) was proving to be seriously ineffective for many students.

Now, we fast forward to the second decade of the 21st century, and Response to Intervention (RTI) has come into its own. In schools and districts throughout the United States, children and adolescents who formerly would have been assigned to special education classes are finding that their academic problems and deficiencies have been lessened and overcome due to appropriate and effective intervention. Within effective RTI programs, those youngsters who need and deserve special education instruction are now being served by expert teachers in settings that are better designed to meet their needs.

However, this has not been the case for many students who are English learners (ELs), students whose home culture differs from the ways of school and whose home language differs from the language of instruction. Too many English learners are still being referred for special education services, regardless of whether they have disabilities, in large part because many classroom teachers are ill prepared to meet their language and academic needs. In other cases, English learners are denied special education services because it is assumed their learning problems are due to language proficiency. These students

languish without appropriate assistance either because of low expectations or because it is thought that they just need more time to learn English.

This book has been written to assist teachers and administrators to better meet the needs of this increasing group of students in U.S. schools, and to help educators design effective RTI programs that provide the appropriate type of instruction that English learners need and deserve in elementary and secondary schools.

The book is organized into seven chapters that include the following;

- **Chapter 1, What Is RTI for English Learners?** In this chapter, we introduce Response to Intervention and discuss its purposes, goals, and components, especially as they relate to English learners.

- **Chapter 2, The Big Picture** This chapter focuses on linguistic and academic issues for English learners, including educational, socioeconomic, and cultural factors that impact student success.

- **Chapter 3, Tier 1: What Is Best Practice for Teaching English Learners?** In this chapter, we discuss best instructional practices for Tier 1 for English learners, including the SIOP® Model.

- **Chapter 4, Tier 2 Interventions for English Learners.** Within the RTI framework, Dr. Cara Richards-Tutor discusses appropriate and effective Tier 2 interventions for English learners, including assessments, Curriculum Based Measurements (CBM), and programmatic decisions that need to be made for individual students.

- **Chapter 5, Tier 3 Interventions for English Learners.** A discussion of intensive interventions for Tier 3 are offered for English learners in this chapter. Differences in English learners are explored, and suggestions are offered about identifying learning disabilities in English learners.

- **Chapter 6, Special Considerations for Secondary English Learners.** In this chapter, we offer specific recommendations about aligning current practices in adolescent literacy with RTI programs for English learners in middle, junior, and high schools.

- **Chapter 7, Successes and Barriers to Effective RTI Implementation.** Guidelines for successful RTI as well as suggestions for overcoming barriers are presented in this chapter. Specifically, we offer questions to guide RTI for English learners. Also, frequently asked questions are addressed.

- **Appendixes and Glossary.** Pertinent text from IDEA 2004 is found in Appendix A. The SIOP® Protocol is included in Appendix B. A glimpse into an effective classroom, along with examples of student writing, are provided in Appendix C. Some student scenarios for reflection and discussion are found in Appendix D. The Glossary includes terminology for both RTI and second language acquisition.

acknowledgments

We acknowledge and thank our reviewers for this book, including Vickie Damon, Renton School District, Renton, WA; Veronica Giles, Bair Middle School, Sunrise, FL; Melissa McKenzie, Instructional Resource Center, Baton Rouge, LA; Karla Stone, Robbinsdale Area Schools, New Hope, MN; and Mirta Silvia Torres, Lee County Public Schools, Fort Myers, FL. Their suggestions and ideas have enhanced our thinking and the recommendations we make in this book. We offer great appreciation to our contributors. Our colleague and friend, Dr. Cara Richards-Tutor, Associate Professor of Special Education at California State University, Long Beach, shared her expertise in the area of intervention in the writing of Chapter 4. Mardell Nash generously provided a practitioner's perspective for this book. Her dedication to providing the best education for every student is unsurpassed. We are also grateful for the ongoing support, advice, and guidance from our colleague, Dr. Claude Goldenberg, Stanford University. As always, we feel very fortunate to have Aurora Martínez as our editor, and we thank her for ongoing advice, support, and friendship. Finally, we offer special appreciation to our co-author, co-researcher, and dear friend, Dr. Deborah Short, from the Center for Applied Linguistics and Academic Language Research & Training.

je, mev

What Is RTI for English Learners?

The extent to which students are connecting to what they are learning, how they are learning it, and who they are learning it with appears to play a central role in how well they do in school.

Suarez-Orozco, Suarez-Orozco, & Todorova, 2008, p. 42

Response to Intervention (RTI) is an instructional delivery model that is designed to identify at-risk learners early and provide appropriate services to them. When considering English learners (ELs), we need to pay attention to how we provide instruction (and intervention) to them, who provides this instruction, and how these students learn in order to achieve positive academic outcomes.

According to the National Center on Response to Intervention, RTI "integrates assessment and intervention within a multi-level prevention system to maximize student achievement and to reduce behavior problems. With RTI, schools identify students at risk for poor learning outcomes, monitor student progress, provide evidence-based interventions and adjust the intensity and nature of those interventions depending on a student's responsiveness, and identify students with learning disabilities." http://www.rti4success.org/

In this chapter we will unpack this definition and discuss the various aspects of RTI with special attention given to English learners.

RTI Is an Opportunity

There is growing concern about how to best serve culturally and linguistically diverse students, particularly English learners who are encountering new, challenging content in a new language. High dropout rates—particularly among Latinos, overall poor academic performance, and disproportionate representation of English learners in special education classes (both over- and under-representation) are some of the realities that contribute to this concern. When implemented well, RTI may be an effective solution to providing the education these students need and deserve.

RTI may be viewed as an overarching conceptual framework that guides the entire school improvement process for all students. The specific purpose of RTI is to reduce the number of students who experience academic and behavior problems, including those who eventually become labeled as "disabled." It was founded on the principles that (a) all children can learn when provided with appropriate, effective instruction and (b) most academic difficulties can be prevented with early identification of need followed by immediate intervention (Echevarria & Hasbrouck, 2009; Fuchs & Deshler, 2007).

Study of human development confirms that all individuals can and will learn under the right conditions. RTI shifts the focus away from the child having a "problem" and onto the learning conditions of the classroom and school. We want to create a learning environment that promotes linguistic and cognitive development using materials, teaching methods, and settings that will facilitate learning for each student. However, early identification of learning difficulties is key (Smith & Tyler, 2010; Tucker & Sornson, 2007; Vaughn, Wanzek, Woodruff, & Linan-Thompson, 2007; Vellutino, Scanlon, & Zhang, 2007). Alba Ortiz, an expert in the field of bilingual special education says, "RTI may help us more quickly identify other factors contributing to low performance. It's important to respond early. You sometimes see third graders referred to special education, but once you examine their records, you realize they have been struggling with language since kindergarten. The more time passes, the harder it is to tell ESL issues from learning disabilities" (Council for Exceptional Children, 2008, p. 2).

Although you may be tempted to consider RTI the latest "new thing" schools are required to do, we suggest that it should be viewed as an opportunity to use a school's or

a district's existing resources, programs, personnel, effective teaching practices, and assessments in a comprehensive way to offer an optimal learning environment for all students. Well implemented RTI establishes a closer working relationship among professionals who are engaged in the education of our most at-risk students.

Historically, when students experienced academic difficulty or behavior problems, the most common response was to wait until the problem was acute enough—until students fell far behind or until some students had a long, documented history of behavior issues—and then they would be referred to special education programs. Over the past 25 years, educators have proposed and experimented with a number of alternative approaches to strengthening the academic achievement of low-performing students as well as identifying more accurately students with learning disabilities (Fuchs & Deshler, 2007; Gersten & Dimino, 2006; Marston et al., 2007). Most recently, RTI has emerged as a more effective process for serving the needs of students with academic and/or behavioral concerns than the traditional "wait to fail" or "identify-test-qualify-place" procedure. Advocates were successful in having RTI included in the Individuals with Disabilities Education Improvement Act of 2004 (IDEA 2004) so that districts have a choice in how they attend to struggling learners (see Appendix A for IDEA Regulations).

Across the country, states and districts require elements of RTI that may vary slightly from one another, but essentially all RTI approaches contain the components seen in Figure 1.1. Some districts prefer to call the process by other names such as "response to instruction" to highlight the important role of teaching. In this example, it is called RTI^2 emphasizing both instruction and intervention.

As you can see in the graphic depiction of the RTI process (Figure 1.2), RTI begins with solid, evidence-based instruction in the general education classroom provided by a highly qualified teacher with regular assessment of student progress. The whole intent of RTI is to move away from looking at poor learning outcomes as indicating there is something wrong with the student and instead to think about what the teacher needs to do to make the student successful. It may be helpful to consider the process "responsiveness of instruction" (Hiebert, Stewart, & Uzicanin, 2010) which rightly places responsibility for student improvement on teaching methods, materials, grouping, pace, and so forth. In the case of English learners, we propose that the SIOP® Model (Sheltered Instruction Observation

---

FIGURE 1.1 *Core Components of RTI^2: Response to Instruction and Intervention*

1. High-quality classroom instruction
2. Research-based instruction
3. Universal screening
4. Continuous classroom monitoring
5. Research-based interventions
6. Progress monitoring during instruction and interventions
7. Fidelity of program implementation
8. Staff development and collaboration
9. Parent involvement
10. Specific learning disability determination

Source: http://www.cde.ca.gov/ci/cr/ri/rticorecomponents.asp

FIGURE 1.2 *A Three-tiered Model of RTI for English Learners*

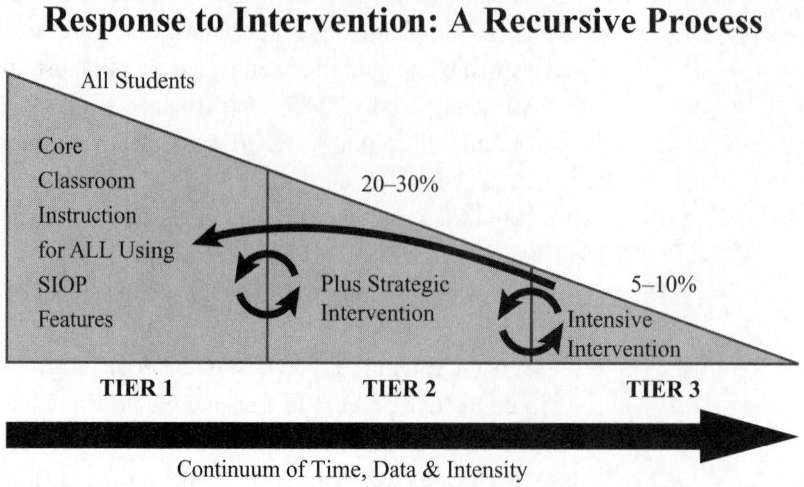

Response to Intervention: A Recursive Process

All Students

Core
Classroom
Instruction
for ALL Using
SIOP
Features

20–30%

5–10%

Plus Strategic
Intervention

Intensive
Intervention

TIER 1   **TIER 2**   **TIER 3**

Continuum of Time, Data & Intensity

Source: Modified from: Echevarria, J., & Hasbrouck, J. (2009). *Response to intervention and English learners* (CREATE Brief). Washington, DC: Center for Research on the Educational Achievement and Teaching of English Language Learners.

Protocol) is the most effective approach to general education instruction because it has been shown to improve the achievement of English learners (Echevarria, Short, & Powers, 2006; Echevarria, et al., in press; Honigsfeld & Cohan, 2008; McIntyre, et al., in press; Short, Fidelman, & Louguit, 2009) and native English speakers (Echevarria, Richards, Canges, & Francis, 2009) when implemented with fidelity.

Sheltered instruction is a way of teaching that uses strategies and techniques to make instruction comprehensible for learners while at the same time promotes academic language development. The SIOP® Model is a lesson planning and delivery system that is comprised of 8 components, each of which reflects research-based practices that should be used systematically and regularly in the general education classroom, as discussed in detail in Chapter 3. Many of these practices are widely known, such as scaffolding, differentiating instruction, providing clear instructions and explanations, using repetition, creating opportunities for oral language practice around meaningful text, and so forth, but they are not consistently practiced in every lesson. The SIOP® Model is a way to ensure that best practices become habitual.

In each tier of the RTI process, instruction and intervention must be tailored to meet the unique needs of English learners. In Santa Rosa, California, SIOP® training for all teachers is part of their LEAP (Local Educational Agency Plan). Staff members at Curriculum and Instruction, Grades 7–12, say, "Having SIOP® as a key component in our LEAP means that we have committed to embed SIOP® at all levels of RTI intervention." In terms of student outcomes, at one middle school where SIOP® is fully implemented, the administration reports having fewer students in intervention (Tier 3), although because they have a large majority of English learners, Tier 2 is still used to provide extra time for support for those students who need it. In addition, student test scores are continuing to rise as teachers have continued to deepen their implementation of the SIOP®.

A brief description of the program is found in Figure 1.3 along with their SIOP® planning template.

FIGURE 1.3 *Santa Rosa Program Description and Planning Template*

In Tier 1, we are in the process of training all middle school and high school content area teachers in the SIOP® Model as well as all classroom teachers in elementary school, since so many of our higher CELDT [language proficiency] level English learners are dispersed throughout the core classes. We have trained all of our administrators using [observation] guides and have embedded language in the guides that serve to develop understanding of the SIOP® features.

Of all our strategic teachers (Tier 2) in English/Language Arts (ELA) nearly all are SIOP® trained. We hold trainings for that cohort three times per year to discuss key components of the SIOP® Model to support these students: Lesson Preparation, Building Background (specifically academic vocabulary development), Strategies, Interaction, and Review and Assessment (particularly as it relates to ongoing checks for understanding).

In our district, Tier 3 includes special education, and intensive ELA and Math classes. Currently, most of our Intensive teachers are trained in SIOP®. In addition, so are many of our Special Education teachers. We will be training more Special Education teachers as a cohort this year.

SANTA ROSA CITY SCHOOLS
Excellence is our Common Ground

S - Specific & Strategic
M - Measurable
A - Attainable
R - Results-oriented
T - Time-bound

SIOP®

SMART Plan

School: _____ Team: _____ Date: _____

Team Members Present:

Content Objective: *As a school team, to develop the implementation of the SIOP® model at our site.*

Language Objectives: *To discuss the steps and resources needed to begin a long-term, systematic SIOP® implementation at the site level. To identify the key qualities of a SIOP® coach and the support provided to the Coach from the District SIOP® team.*

<u>INITIAL ACTION PLAN TO SET-UP IMPLEMENTATION TEAM</u>

<u>Site team will identify:</u>

Result	Timeframe	
SIOP® Facilitator		
Core teacher group		
Resources		

(Continued)

FIGURE 1.3 *Continued*

Result	Timeframe	
Timeline		
Measures for data analysis		
Meeting format and times		

SIOP® Team ACTION PLAN

Objectives:

Action Steps	Who	Timeframe	Results
What steps or activities will be initiated to achieve this goal?	Who will be responsible for initiating or sustaining the action steps?	What is a realistic timeframe for each phase of the activity?	What evidence will you present that you are making progress toward your goal?

FIGURE 1.3 *Continued*

Principal's Comments

_____

_____

_____

_____

_____

_____

_____

_____

As you can see in Figure 1.2, RTI is a recursive process, not a linear one. Students move in and out of intervention as needed for specific skill development in language, reading, writing, or math. For example, a student may require Tier 2 intervention in math, but also receive Tier 3 intervention in reading. The duration of intervention and the decision about whether a student is dismissed from intervention and returned to the general education classroom for 100% of their day depends on the needs of the learner. Even when students receive intervention, it is important to remember that typically, intervention is a small part of the day that focuses on building specific skills to enhance learning in the general education classroom. Intervention is skill specific, but for the majority of the school day, English learners are in general education and should be engaged in rich, meaningful discussion and activities around text. Teaching techniques are used that encourage active participation and provide students with the support they need to be successful in each lesson. Even if English learners receive Tier 2 and Tier 3 intervention, instruction in their general education classroom must reflect best practice for English learners.

Using RTI as a "prevention system," a teacher's intent is to create a learning environment that will catch difficulties early and provide the type of instruction and modifications that will in some cases ameliorate those difficulties and in other cases support learning so that all students are successful. In either situation, the goal is maximizing student achievement and reducing behavior problems. Unfortunately, this is not always the experience of struggling students and their families. As one parent recently emailed:

> If only we could get everyone who is involved in the education of our children to think about what the adults need to do to help students succeed instead of labeling children who struggle as defective and in need of fixing. My daughter has a nonverbal learning disability, which affects every aspect of her life (and mine), so I am a veteran of the special ed process. Our school district has been very good to us overall, and I am grateful for the special ed services that Cassie receives. She needs them in order to be successful in the general ed classroom. But we have encountered too many teachers along the way who seemed to feel that the onus was on Cassie to learn to do things their way rather than figuring out how they could adapt their ways to better meet Cassie's needs.

FIGURE 1.4 *What RTI Is/Is Not*

RTI is A/An . . .

- Process that begins by focusing on effective instruction in the general education classroom. Emphasis is on what the teacher needs to do to make the student successful, providing instructional intervention in reading and mathematics, immediately upon student need.
- Data-driven process (using progress monitoring and assessments) to improve reading and math.
- General education-led effort implemented within the general education system, coordinated with all other services including special education, Title I, ESL, Migrant Education, Reading First, School Improvement.
- Alternative approach to the diagnosis of a Learning Disability.
- Process that determines if the child responds to scientific, research-based intervention as a part of the evaluation procedures.

RTI is NOT A/An . . .

- System for identifying what is "wrong" with the student.
- Pre-referral system only.
- Holding place for students with behavior and academic challenges.
- Special education placement.
- Curriculum.
- Additional period of ELD, math, or reading.
- Adjective (to describe students, teachers, or classes).

Our focus should be on finding out what students CAN do and searching for what type of instruction, modification, or accommodation works for them, regardless of whether they have been diagnosed with a language/learning disability. Figure 1.4 shows that there are a number of misconceptions about the purpose of RTI and its function in a school or district. It is not a "new way" to refer students to special education, as some teachers have called it. Some aspects of the RTI process may be similar to conducting and documenting pre-referral interventions, but RTI is not a path toward special education placement. In fact, it can prevent students from being referred unnecessarily for costly services if what they need is specific skills development. RTI is not a classroom set aside where students are sent when they experience behavior and academic problems; it is an approach that involves all school personnel. It is a schoolwide process, and the success of students is the responsibility of everyone, not one teacher in one location. An RTI process searches for what will work most effectively for individual students; it is more than simply providing an additional period of English language development (ELD), math, or reading and it is more than a curriculum developed for "intervention." Finally, please do not use RTI as an adjective to describe students, teachers, or classes (e.g., Mr. Cavale, the RTI teacher, or Gabriela is RTI). Using the term as an adjective relegates the responsibility for successful RTI to one specific teacher or classroom and unnecessarily labels students who receive services.

RTI is about assessing students, monitoring their progress, and providing the kinds of instruction and intervention they need to learn the skills or behaviors required to be successful in the classroom. It's not all about intervention – it is about focusing on effective

instruction in the general education classroom, and then considering interventions if students continue to struggle. We want to prevent problems from occurring at the first sign of risk.

RTI Definition Unpacked

Multi-tier Approach

Although most commonly referred to as a three-tiered approach, it is more accurate to say RTI is multi-tiered because there may be more than three tiers in an RTI process (Vaughn & Klinger, 2007). Typically, the tiers represent the following: Tier 1 is the general education classroom and core curriculum that all students receive. Tier 2 provides intervention for qualified students that supplements the core curriculum and classroom practice. Tier 2 services do not absolve general education teachers of responsibility for providing modifications to ensure student success. (Later in this chapter we will discuss specific modifications and adaptations that take place in Tier 1.) Tier 3 involves more intensive, individualized intervention and may or may not include students with identified disabilities who have an Individualized Education Plan (IEP). In some models, students with IEPs receive special education services in Tier 4.

RTI should be thought of as a continuum of services that increases in intensity based on student need, and is recursive in nature; students move in and out of tiered services as needed. The number of levels or tiers offered is not as important as the use of an approach that works best for students.

Assessment and Intervention

The first sentence of the National Center on Response to Intervention definition, "(RTI) integrates assessment and intervention within a multi-level prevention system to maximize student achievement and to reduce behavior problems," illustrates the relationship between assessment and instruction or intervention. One key element of effective RTI is using assessment to measure student progress and employing the results to inform the type of intervention needed as well as direct the focus of instruction in the general education classroom (Fuchs & Fuchs, 2007). As Olson et al. (2007) remark, "After all, the primary purpose of assessment should always be improving student learning" (p. 117).

Identify Areas of Concern and Monitor Progress

Early identification and support for students at risk for poor learning outcomes and behavior problems is critical, especially given the fact mentioned previously that in the past, schools waited for students to fall significantly behind their peers before services were provided (Council for Exceptional Children, 2008; Gersten & Dimino, 2006; Tucker & Sornson, 2007; Vaughn, Wanzek, Woodruff, & Linan-Thompson, 2007; Vellutino, Scanlon, & Zhang, 2007). The RTI process begins with high-quality instruction and universal screening of all children in the general education classroom. Universal screening is used to determine the performance or skill level of all students, and those who show deficits

have a diagnostic evaluation to determine the exact nature and scope of the problem. Data for the diagnosis may be obtained from the following sources:

- End of unit assessments (from the core curriculum)
- Leveled running records
- Orthographic assessments
- Anecdotal notes (e.g., doesn't follow directions)

Remember that any diagnostic tools or standardized assessments must consider the student's English language proficiency. Imagine having important decisions being made about your ability and your potential success based on a test given in a language in which you are not fluent!

Even with language proficiency being taken into consideration, there will be learners who continue to struggle; they would be provided Tier 2 intervention (discussed in Chapter 4). Early intervention is critical, although some researchers have suggested that as many as 50% of first graders identified as at-risk through one-time universal screening may make satisfactory progress throughout their first grade year without Tier 2 intervention. Weekly progress monitoring for five weeks helped to more accurately identify those students who needed intervention. The researchers recommended that a combination of universal screening (to identify at-risk learners) and short-term progress monitoring (to identify students for Tier 2) be used to avoid targeting children who, given more time with high quality instruction, will not require unnecessary and costly Tier 2 services (Fuchs & Deshler, 2007). This approach may be particularly useful for English learners since language acquisition requires time; some of these students may make progress over time with effective instruction and careful progress monitoring.

Interventions continue at increasing levels of intensity as needed to accelerate students' rate of learning. Progress is closely monitored to assess both the learning rate and the level of performance of individual students. Tier 2 and Tier 3 intervention is intended to be short term, lasting a specified number of weeks. Most students will be dismissed from Tier 2 services once they have acquired the skills they need. Students receiving Tier 3 intervention may need intensive support for a longer period of time, after which they may move to Tier 2 intervention for less intensive support. Some students may be dismissed from intervention and receive all instruction in their general education classroom. (See Figure 1.2.)

It is important to remember that Tier 2 and Tier 3 interventions are not designed for students who are just having difficulty in meeting grade-level standards such as interpreting tables and graphs in social studies or finding a theme in a novel. Interventions are for students who have difficulty with key skills that impact more global success in the content area.

For students who have difficulty in meeting specific standards, RTI provides an opportunity for educators to examine the general education classroom to ensure that research-validated instruction, such as the kind presented in Chapter 3, is in place and that teachers are meeting their students' needs. Some general practices for improving students' performance that supplement teaching include the following:

- Conferencing with a parent or guardian
- Conducting a health screening to check vision and hearing
- Moving a student to another seat or to a carrel to reduce distractions

- Allowing another student to translate using a student's native language
- Designing a behavior or academic contract with a student and/or family
- Reducing the number of math problems or questions in any subject area for a student
- Conferencing with the student, using an interpreter if needed
- Providing the student with assistive technology
- Adjusting the level of difficulty of an assignment
- Providing sentence frames, outlines of a text or lecture, or other scaffolds
- Permitting students to complete an assignment using their native language
- Giving a student extended time to complete an assignment or take a test

These would *not* be considered interventions; these are part of a teacher's repertoire for differentiating instruction as needed. These are the kinds of things "good" teachers do because they know these modifications will facilitate their students' learning. (See Figure 1.5 to see the distinction between accommodations, modifications, and interventions.) However, it is still important to provide documentation so that a comprehensive record of the student's education is created. The Record of Modifications and/or Accommodations (Figure 1.6) is useful for a number of purposes including:

1. It provides a record of what was tried previously, for how long, and its effectiveness with the student that teachers can refer to as they think about how to modify instruction.

FIGURE 1.5 *Clarifying RTI Terms*

Accommodations	*Modifications*	*Interventions*
Use assistive technology	Simplify directions, providing picture support, if needed	Form small groups consisting of students with similar academic profiles (3–5 students, depending on intensity required)
Tape-record reading assignment for homework and/or review	Reduce number of correct responses required (e.g., math problems)	Focus on specific skills, e.g., fluency and comprehension
Give a test orally so student can express knowledge without reading and/or writing	Slow the pace of instruction	Develop targeted vocabulary, using words in context with sufficient repetition
Provide peer tutoring	Adjust the level of difficulty of an assignment	Select materials appropriate for student's ability
Move the student's seat to reduce distractions	Give an outline for an assignment (in the native language, if needed)	Provide immediate, explicit feedback on responses
Pair student with a partner who speaks the student's native language	Provide sentence frames for oral participation and writing tasks	Increase intensity by lowering number of students in the group, providing intervention more frequently, and moving at a brisk pace

FIGURE 1.6 *Record of Modifications and/or Accommodations*

Student (Last Name) _____ First Name_____

Teacher Name _____

Modifications/Accommodations *Note date(s) used, and outcome*	*K*	*1*	*2*	*3*	*4*	*5*
Access to Taped Books/Text						
Adapted Texts						
Assessment by Psychologist (informal)						
Behavior Contract						
Classroom Instructional Aide						
Cross Age Tutoring						

FIGURE 1.6 *Continued*

Modifications/Accommodations *Note date(s) used, and outcome*	K	1	2	3	4	5
English Language Development/ESL						
Extended Time to Complete Assignment						
Health Screening						
Homework Helper						
In-School Counseling (Straight Talk, etc.)						
Kids Korner/Homework Time						
Language Proficiency Assessment						
Learning Specialist Support						

(Continued)

FIGURE 1.6 *Continued*

Modifications/Accommodations	K	1	2	3	4	5
Note date(s) used, and outcome						
Modified Assignments						
Modified Class Assessments						
Parent Contact Re: Absences/Tardies						
Peer Tutoring						
Primary Language Instruction						
Private Tutoring						
Psychologist Observation						

FIGURE 1.6 *Continued*

Modifications/Accommodations	K	1	2	3	4	5
Note date(s) used, and outcome						
Retention						
RSP (Special Education Support)						
Small Group Math Instruction						
Small Group Reading Instruction						
Reading Intervention						
Special Classroom Seating						
Multidisciplinary Team Meeting						

(Continued)

FIGURE 1.6 *Continued*

Modifications/Accommodations	K	1	2	3	4	5
Note date(s) used, and outcome						
Student Planner Monitored						
Summer School						
Tutoring from Adult Volunteer						

2. It provides a historical record for teachers in subsequent grades that might guide their instructional decisions.

3. A record of Tier 1 classroom modifications would help inform decisions if a student is considered for Tier 2 intervention.

4. The form becomes part of a comprehensive record that might be used as part of the student's evaluation if the student is considered for Tier 3 intervention.

5. The record may be useful when conferencing with parents to show the type of things that work well or to provide an account of modifications that were provided before their child was referred for more intensive intervention.

Remember that screening and progress monitoring are done for a purpose: to make changes for those students identified as at-risk. So, we conduct screening and progress monitoring—and then do something about it. Students who make progress are moved out of groups, which creates more time for the ones who need it (Vanderwood & Nam, 2007).

Provide Evidence-based Interventions

Intervention in Tier 2 is the use of a research-validated program that supplements the core curriculum. We adjust the intensity and nature of those interventions depending on a student's responsiveness. As previously mentioned, RTI begins with high-quality instruction in the general education classroom, where teachers make numerous individual modifications to the instructional program in order to support each student's achievement. Even in this context, there will be students who have not mastered the critical skills they need to perform well academically across curricular areas. Therefore, in addition to regular classroom

instruction, approximately 20%–30% of learners may need additional intervention. Specific Tier 2 interventions are discussed in detail in Chapter 4 and may include small group reading and writing instruction using text leveled for difficulty. For English learners, it is important to use interesting, meaningful materials and to make connections to what they know.

Although there is limited research about which specific interventions are effective with English learners, it appears that some of the same interventions that are used with native English speakers can be used to improve the outcomes for English learners who receive core literacy instruction in English (Vanderwood & Nam, 2007).

Identify Learning Disabilities

As we have mentioned previously, the under- and overidentification of English learners and other diverse students for special education services makes RTI appealing for reaching more accurate eligibility decisions. RTI, if implemented well, takes into consideration, during referral and eligibility decision-making, the classroom context including quality of instruction (particularly with regard to early literacy), teacher qualification to teach English learners, students' language proficiency match to materials and instruction, and other factors that have not typically been considered. (We discuss these issues in more depth in the next chapter.) Instead, school personnel have "seemed quick to attribute a child's struggles to internal deficits or the home environment" (Klinger, Sorrels, & Barrera, 2007, p. 225).

If English learners have received high-quality instruction in general education that is research-validated for ELs (Chapter 3), if their language proficiency and sociocultural context has been considered (Chapter 2), and if appropriate intervention has been tried and well documented (Chapters 4 and 5), yet they are not making progress with appropriate intervention (and other factors have been excluded as influences on their learning), then identification of a learning disability should be considered.

As one veteran teacher commented about identifying students who have not responded to intervention, "Be sure you've tried everything before referring a student for testing. It is very costly in terms of money, time, and labor. The special education teacher isn't teaching while she's testing; the school psychologist can't do other things when testing. You want to avoid unnecessary referrals." Well-implemented RTI holds promise for providing English learners with adequate opportunity to learn so that we can more accurately differentiate between those who do and do not have learning disabilities and provide appropriate special education services to students who are eligible.

RTI Models

In addition to variations in the number of tiers used to deliver RTI services, schools also use different approaches in implementation, such as problem-solving, standard treatment protocol, and hybrid approaches (Echevarria & Hasbrouck, 2009). Although the RTI components (for example, universal screening and tiered model) look similar under both problem-solving and standard treatment protocol, the approaches vary in how interventions are implemented.

Standard Treatment Protocol

In the standard treatment protocol, one standard intervention is given for a fixed duration to a group of students with similar needs. This approach assumes that providing the same

research-based intervention to similarly grouped students introduces a level of quality control (National Association of State Directors of Special Education, 2005).

For example, in Roosevelt School, students who test at the "struggling" level are automatically placed in one hour of supplemental literacy (or math) instruction. This Tier 2 intervention is in addition to general education literacy instruction. Students who test two grade levels below are placed in Tier 3, which is intensive intervention (Tier 4 is special education). Tier 3 curriculum and instruction typically supplants the core curriculum because it is intended to offer students something different to move them at an accelerated pace.

One drawback is relying on assessment results to automatically place students in Tier 2 and Tier 3 interventions. With English learners, some assessments are questionable and may not be accurate for this population (Figueroa, 2002; Hosp & Madyun, 2007; Ortiz & Yates, 2002; Vanderwood & Nam, 2007).

In addition, teachers may not provide adequate modifications and accommodations in the student's general education classroom because they have come to rely on automatically sending struggling students to intervention. There is not the level of support that problem-solving teams provide to assist teachers with ideas for modifications, instructional techniques and strategies, progress monitoring, and interpreting data.

Finally, we run the risk of beginning to think of RTI as a curriculum that students are plugged into rather than considering all options for making the student successful. Ultimately, the teacher always provides the intervention, not the materials.

Problem-Solving Model

In the problem-solving model, a team of practitioners identifies and evaluates the problems of an individual student and designs and implements flexible interventions to meet that student's needs. This model typically has four stages: problem identification, problem analysis, plan implementation, and plan evaluation. This model assumes that no one intervention is effective for all students (National Association of State Directors of Special Education, 2005). A key feature in successful RTI models is teachers working together and examining data as a team (Haagar & Mahdavi, 2007). This team approach offers the possibility of reducing the likelihood that student will be misplaced. The team examines data and considers lots of possibilities. Student progress is constantly monitored and the team takes the results and discusses options.

For example, in Bellevue School, when the classroom teacher is concerned about a student, he or she goes to the site-based council and discusses the student with the other members (problem identification and problem analysis) (see Figure 1.7, RTI Record). They offer suggestions for classroom modifications and accommodations that are specific for addressing the concerns about the student. The teacher goes back and tries some of the ideas suggested (plan implementation), documenting the duration and outcome. The team examines the documentation and makes appropriate decisions about how well the suggestions were implemented (plan evaluation). For some students, the classroom modifications the teacher implemented provide the support the students needed and the process ends. If student progress isn't adequate after receiving modifications/ accommodations, the team conducts further problem-solving. The student would most likely be recommended for Tier 2 intervention that supplements classroom instruction. A student who is in Tier 2 will require a detailed plan about the intervention to be implemented. For example, in addition to the core curriculum and methods already in place, a

FIGURE 1.7 *RTI Record: A Problem-Solving Approach*

RTI Record

Student: _____ Grade: ___ DOB: _____ Date of Meeting: _____

Teacher: _____ School: _____

Reading: _____ Math: _____ English Proficiency Level: _____

Home Language: _____

Area(s) of Difficulty (Check)

    ☐ Articulation   ☐ Writing   ☐ Social Emotional

    ☐ Language   ☐ Math   ☐ History/Health Concerns

    ☐ Listening   ☐ Motor Skills   ☐ Attendance

    ☐ Reading   ☐ Academic English   ☐ Behavior

Specific Difficulty _____

Student's Strengths _____

Teacher Accommodations and/or Modifications (use a separate line for each

modification/accommodation) _____

Date Began: _____ Duration: _____

Outcome: _____

Specific Interventions Developed by RTI Site Council

Describe the intervention(s) _____

Frequency _____

Duration _____

How will effectiveness be measured? _____

_____

Date of RTI Site Council Follow-up Meeting: _____

Summary of intervention effectiveness (after _____ weeks)

_____

student will meet with the teacher in a small group three times a week (frequency). During that time, they will work for 30 minutes (intensity) on phonemic awareness for a period of 6–12 weeks (duration of the intervention). This team problem-solving process continues as the student continues to experience difficulty and is used when making decisions in both general education and special education, creating a well-integrated system of instruction and intervention guided by student outcome data.

    The drawback of this model is that it is time- and labor-intensive and requires a level of sophistication in terms of understanding instruction for English learners, pinpointing

appropriate intervention based on specific student need, accurate data collection and interpretation, and fidelity of intervention for it to be effective.

Hybrid Approaches

As mentioned, the two approaches are not necessarily mutually exclusive. In some cases a combination or hybrid of the two approaches is used; both types of interventions may be provided within each tier, based on student needs.

Although there are several ways a school might implement RTI to best serve the needs of its students, RTI should be a schoolwide framework for efficiently allocating resources to improve student outcomes (http://www.rtinetwork.org/Learn/What/ar/WhatIsRTI) and the process must be implemented with fidelity to be effective.

Making RTI Work

To begin using an RTI approach or to enhance the effectiveness of the one you are currently using, there are a number of issues to consider.

First, fidelity is critical. In education research, fidelity is defined as the degree to which an intervention or model of instruction is implemented as it was originally designed to be implemented (Gresham, MacMillan, Beebe-Frankenberger, & Bocian, 2000). Fidelity in the RTI process involves:

- **Instruction**—All students, including English learners, receive systematic, research-based teaching that is consistent and effective. Many districts commit to professional development to ensure that all teachers are highly qualified for teaching content area subjects as well as understanding effective instruction for English learners.

- **Intervention**—For students who struggle, intervention is implemented with high fidelity and in the specific way the approach was intended. Intervention involves research-validated instructional techniques and implementation approximates as closely as possible the original model used in the research.

- **RTI process**—Assessments are used accurately for benchmark/screening, skill diagnosis, and progress monitoring. Data are used effectively for making decisions about placement, instruction, and program evaluation. These aspects of RTI cross all tiers and are essential.

Second, an important aspect of effective RTI is documentation. Developing a comprehensive record of student performance—and how the *school* responded to assessment data—will provide critical information for decision-making. Figure 1.7 shows a sample form that may be used to document initial concern (based on universal screening and/or teacher recommendation), the kind of modifications the teacher used in the classroom with the student, and the recommended intervention, duration, and outcome. This form reflects a problem-solving approach to RTI as noted by the "RTI Site Council."

Third, effective RTI requires administrative support to make it happen well. In Figure 1.8 we have provided some questions for administrators to consider for implementing high-quality RTI. Teachers and other school personnel need to be aware of effective instructional practices for all students, including the research for teaching English learners

FIGURE 1.8 *Questions to Consider: Administrative Support*

- Are you supervising the RTI process by going into classrooms, checking lesson plans, observing instruction with English learners, reviewing data, and monitoring intervention?
- Are you using all your staff effectively by encouraging collaboration between general educators, ESL and bilingual personnel, special educators, and other specialists?
- Have you provided adequate time for teachers to discuss at-risk students? Where in the schedule could you fit that in? Is there a specific room to discuss RTI? (Not the lunch room!)
- Do you oversee the forms needed for the process? (For example, Are they updated, accessible for teachers, enough copies?) Do the forms specifically address issues related to English learners? (e.g., language development, cultural considerations)
- Are your teachers qualified to work effectively with English learners?
- Are the student assessments used appropriate for English learners?
- What kind of professional development do your teachers need? Do you have a plan that prioritizes topics? (e.g., effective instruction for English learners, understanding second language acquisition, implementing the RTI process, and how to monitor progress and interpret data)
- Have you established relationships with culturally diverse families? Have you made sufficient effort to involve them in the RTI process as valued partners?
- Are you following through on certain students who require it? Do you contact families who aren't following through with agreements? Is someone checking on a student who has poor attendance?

presented in Chapter 3. In addition, development of procedures for accurate assessment of students, and collection and interpretation of data is critical since these results will be used to inform instructional decisions. Figure 1.9 provides some questions for teachers to consider during the planning phase when developing assessments for students as well as for consideration when collecting student data. We want to create optimal conditions for students to demonstrate their knowledge and skills. Collaboration among school personnel facilitates understanding of student data results and increases the likelihood that the results will be interpreted accurately and used effectively. As the questions for administrators imply (Figure 1.8), time needs to be set aside for collaboration.

Finally, effective RTI requires substantial professional development. Districts should create a long-term professional development plan that addresses fidelity of instruction,

FIGURE 1.9 *Questions for Teachers to Consider: Preparing Assessments and Collecting Data*

- Are you giving ample time for the student to complete the task?
- Would another day be advantageous for testing the student because s/he is tired or ill?
- Are you testing in a place with minimal distractions?
- Are you doing the testing yourself, or are you relying on someone unfamiliar with the student?
- Will a tester unfamiliar with the child recognize progress since that person may not be aware of the child's English proficiency level or areas of difficulty, e.g., articulation problems?
- Is the language demand too high for the student's English proficiency level?
- Are you repeating the directions, as needed? Are you checking for understanding? Can the student explain to you what you want him or her to do on the test?
- Does the student need the instructions translated into his/her home language?
- Have you pre-taught the vocabulary of the task you're testing them on?

fidelity of intervention, and implementing all aspects of RTI with fidelity. Professional development needs to be ongoing and sustained to support teachers in:

- Providing high-quality instruction and intervention
- Selecting and accurately administering assessments for benchmark/screening, skill diagnosis, and progress monitoring
- Using assessments for decisions about placement, instruction, and program evaluation

Final Thoughts

Response to Intervention (RTI) is a multi-tier approach to educational decisions about the intensity, frequency, and duration of interventions based on individual student response to instruction. Sometimes we can get caught up in benchmarks, interventions, progress monitoring, and programs and we can lose sight of the individual learner. With English learners, we need to step back and look at the big picture. In the next chapter we will discuss factors that impact learning for English learners and should be part of the discussion whenever an English learner struggles academically or behaviorally.

For Reflection and Discussion

1. In the Standard Treatment Protocol, what is the drawback to relying on assessment results to automatically place students in Tier 2 interventions? What about Tier 3?

2. The students at Cabrillo middle school are supposed to be assessed every four weeks to make sure they are making adequate progress academically. However, due to absenteeism, school activities, teacher apathy, and other factors, the practice isn't consistent. The idea of RTI is to provide a quick response to academic problems, but these students are falling farther behind without interventions, consistent documentation, and progress monitoring. If you were a district administrator in charge of implementing an RTI model, what recommendations would you make to the building administration and staff?

3. Why is fidelity such a critical issue for RTI? How might you ensure that a school staff is implementing the process with fidelity?

chapter 2

The Big Picture

It's never just about the child. They bring with them their cultural histories, their own assumptions about what it means to engage in learning, and native languages that must be understood and valued.

Professor Elizabeth Kozleski

The challenge for English learners is that they are learning rigorous, standards-based content in a language in which they are not yet fully proficient. They attend schools with practices and expectations that they may not understand completely and that may not reflect the values of their home. So, English learners are learning the language of English at the same time they are studying curricular content, learning how to express their ideas, understanding the ways of school, and so forth, through English.

To give you an idea of what it is like to try to make sense of a difficult concept, the following explanation of how to use formulas to convert radians to degrees and back might suffice. Could you explain this formula to a colleague in your own words?

A radian is the measure of an angle that, when drawn as a central angle of a circle, intercepts an arc whose length is equal to the length of the radius of the circle. The length of 1 radius stretches out to a portion of the circle. That portion is 1 radian of the circle. There is a simple formula to convert radians to degrees: 1Π radian $= 180$. Therefore you can easily convert from one unit of measure to the other.

For some of you, the task was easy. For others, you tried with some difficulty to make sense of it, perhaps using your academic background. Some of you undoubtedly disengaged—lost interest immediately and didn't even attempt to decipher the text. Other readers may have been moderately successful in making sense of the text but with lots of energy expended. This task represents the experience of millions of students in our schools every day.

Unfortunately, students also disengage from school for a number of reasons that we will discuss in this chapter.

The intent of this chapter is to help educators understand that in our efforts to assist students in reaching benchmarks, attaining standards, and passing standardized tests, we may lose sight of the whole child. There are myriad influences and realities that impact learning, especially for English learners. Some realities to keep in mind as we discuss the education of English learners throughout this book include:

1. Immigration almost inevitably includes (at least temporarily) issues such as loss of status and difficulty communicating. Students are put in the position of interpreting for their parents, which can impact family roles and lead to feelings of inadequacy. Imagine your own feeling of incompetence if you had to depend on your own child to communicate with officials, doctors, teachers, and other people you encounter in everyday life. In our research, one of the teachers with whom we worked had been a physician in Mexico, yet in the United States was teaching remedial science classes in a rough inner city high school. Over the years we have met many school staff such as teacher aides who held professional positions in their home country.

2. Poverty impacts learning. More than 60% of English learners come from poor families (August & Shanahan, 2006; Garcia & Jensen, 2007). The impact of poverty on learning is significant and includes the following realities for poor children: They have a greater risk of exposure to lead, which causes lower IQ, learning disabilities, and behavior problems; they suffer from hunger and poor nutrition; their parents typically do not engage in talking and reading with them, reducing language development and early literacy opportunities (at 36 months old, the vocabulary of children in professional families is more than double that of children in

families receiving welfare); and they tend not to engage in summer enrichment programs, resulting in reading losses (Barton & Coley, 2009). Poverty is also the largest correlate of reading achievement. The number of students receiving free or reduced-price lunch in a school can provide a fairly accurate estimate about test scores (Cunningham, 2006).

3. Separation from loved ones, even their own parents, can lead to depression, feelings of isolation, and sadness. "The separation of children from their family members during immigration is a complex and long-lasting process that generates lingering long-distance emotional ties" (Suarez-Orozco, Suarez-Orozco, & Todorova, 2008, p. 69).

4. Household and family responsibilities may interfere with education. Low performing students were more than 3 times as likely to report missing school to help with their families than high performing students (Suarez-Orozco, Suarez-Orozco, & Todorova, 2008).

5. Teacher attitudes affect student achievement. Teachers want students to behave in certain ways, and it is well documented that they give higher grades to those students they like and who behave in ways that suit their preference. These attitudes and expectations also extend to parents: Those who have time to participate in school activities are considered interested in their child's education and those who do not participate are deemed uninterested. Thompson (2008) concluded that her study of low-performing schools illustrated "the culture of low expectations and disrespect that prevails in schools that serve many Black and Latino families" (p. 52). When minority students perform poorly on tests and earn low grades, teachers often blame the students and their parents. They attribute poor performance on being lazy, not valuing education, and having parents that don't care (Hale, 2001; Thompson, 2004).

6. The challenges youngsters face when they enter American schools are particularly difficult for those who come during the middle school and high school years. They must not only learn English quickly so they can participate in interpersonal communication with teachers and peers but also acquire enough English to learn rigorous subject matter when instruction is conducted exclusively in English (Valdes, 2001).

We begin this chapter by discussing some issues to keep in the forefront of your mind as you read the remainder of this book. English learners—like all children—come to school with their own experiences, home values, and ideas; they "see" schooling through this lens. We cannot cover all the issues English learners face in this chapter; indeed entire volumes are devoted to their impact on learners (e.g., Cummins, 2000; Glen & de Jong, 1996; Suarez-Orozco, Suarez-Orozco, & Todorova, 2008; Valdes, 2001), but we touch on some sociocultural and linguistic factors that impact learning and some critical issues for educating English learners.

We also discuss how effective schools can help mitigate the outside-of-school factors that impact learning so that English learners are successful. The learning context for English learners presents a unique set of issues, and the RTI process will be more effective when educators are aware of these issues and adjust the process to accommodate these realities. We will discuss in more detail some influences on student learning and point out factors associated with educational success for English learners. We conclude the chapter with a discussion of the important role of parents.

Issues Faced by English Learners in School

Language Proficiency

English proficiency is the greatest predictor of academic success for English learners—more than all other factors combined (Suarez-Orozco, Suarez-Orozco, & Todorova, 2008). When we refer to academic English proficiency, it is more than simply "learning English." The social, conversational speaking ability that one learns through exposure to a language is different from the academic language proficiency required in classroom settings and on standardized tests.

Academic Language. This type of language differs from conversational language and is extremely important since academic English proficiency is highly predictive of academic success. In schools, this distinction is known as BICS (basic interpersonal communicative skills) and CALP (cognitive academic language proficiency), with the latter referred to as academic language (Cummins, 1984; 2000). Academic language is defined in a number of ways, such as the language of the classroom, the language of academic disciplines (science, history, mathematics, literary analysis), and of texts and literature. Academic English is more abstract and decontextualized than conversational English and is not typically found in everyday settings. The ability to perform on multiple choice tests, to extract meaning from written text, and to argue a point verbally and in writing are essential skills for high levels of academic attainment. In fact, oral language proficiency may be even more critical since higher oral language proficiency is significantly correlated with higher grades and even more strongly with achievement test outcomes (Suarez-Orozco, Suarez-Orozco, & Todorova, 2008).

There is general academic language that crosses curricular areas (Coxhead, 2000; Zwiers, 2008) and there are also specific academic language terms associated with each content area. For example, some content specific language in math would include *divisibility, histogram, front-end estimation, unit conversion, variability*, and *expanded notation* (Echevarria, Vogt, & Short, 2010c). Academic language for social studies includes terms such as *conflict, colonization, interpret, relief map, longitude,* and *plateau* (Short, Vogt, & Echevarria, 2010b). Science terms that are specific to that content area include *magnetism, attraction, consumers, investigation, prediction, igneous rock*, and *bar graph* (Short, Vogt, & Echevarria, 2010a). Although English Language Arts (ELA) would seem to have terms for general language development, in reality the study of ELA includes specific terms such as *homographs, characteristics of nonfiction, citations, text features, conjunctions*, and *logical fallacies* (Vogt, Echevarria, & Short, 2010).

Research findings highlight the importance of providing high-quality English language development (ELD) for English learners (August & Shanahan, 2006; Genesee, Lindholm-Leary, Saunders, & Christian, 2006). So, effective teaching includes both content and language objectives in every lesson to ensure that there is an explicit focus on language development along with the topic or skill being taught. Further, ELD may be accelerated by providing a separate period in which the instructional focus is solely on language development (Saunders, Foorman, & Carlson, 2006).

Background Knowledge and Experience

Students come to school with a wealth of knowledge, and their previous cultural, language, and literacy experiences influence their ways of learning. In a classroom with culturally diverse students, the students' background knowledge and experience don't always align with the materials and content of the classroom. Here is an example. This is a high stakes test you must pass. What are these sentences referring to? You have one chance to answer:

1. This type does not have a high cantle.
2. It is designed to provide optimal movement, including classical dressage.
3. A piece of equipment may vary in style based on discipline, but most feature some type of cavesson noseband.
4. Most standards require, as a minimum, jodhpurs.

If you don't have background in English horseback riding, then you most likely did not pass the test! So much of what we understand is based on our background experiences—or lack thereof. English learners are responsible for learning and understanding content that is based on assumptions of common experiences and are, quite literally, foreign to them and their background experiences. Effective instruction for English learners connects new concepts with the students' personal experiences and past learning. When students have knowledge of a topic, they have better recall and are better able to elaborate on the topic than those with limited knowledge of the subject (Chiesi, Spilich, & Voss, 1979).

Cultural Values and Norms

Mere exposure to another culture doesn't change one's own values and behaviors; cultural values are deeply engrained in us, although they may appear in subtle ways. They influence the way we interact with others, make sense of our environment, and deal with conflict; in fact, they permeate every aspect of daily life and the lives of English learners in school.

Cultural norms and values are influenced by a number of factors including one's race or ethnicity, which typically has a profound impact. Figure 2.1 shows some other influences on culture such as the family's religious beliefs and practices, educational level, and socioeconomic status.

English learners' family practices and values don't always map on neatly to school culture, which can create dissonance for English learners and be misinterpreted by education professionals. Some examples of cultural norms and values include notions of modesty and concepts of beauty, ways that language is learned and used, approaches to problem-solving, order of time, and incentives to work (Hamayan, 2006). You may think of a friend (or a spouse!) whose values differ from your own on some of these aspects.

As educators we need to be aware of the way culture influences values and practices, which is why it is critical that professionals knowledgeable about individual students' cultures be part of the decision-making process of RTI. Culturally appropriate interpretation of behavior and of data is mandatory when examining the academic progress of English learners.

FIGURE 2.1 *Influences on Culture*

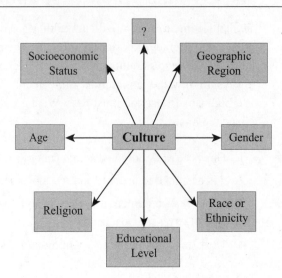

The influences on learning discussed above are at the student level. We now turn to institutional influences, those that impede learning and those that facilitate academic achievement.

Factors Associated with Underachievement

Researchers specializing in the status of English learners and children of immigrants suggest a number of factors that impact these students' well-being (Padron, Waxman, & Rivera, 2002; Rumberger, Gandara, & Merino, 2006; Suarez-Orozco, Suarez-Orozco, & Todorova, 2008).

Lack of Qualified Teachers

Teacher quality is strongly related to student achievement (Darling-Hammond, 2000). English learners, particularly those from low-income backgrounds, continue to have poor academic, social, and postsecondary outcomes (Barton & Coley, 2009; McCardle, et al., 2005). Legislation such as No Child Left Behind (NCLB) and the Individuals With Disabilities Education Improvement Act (IDEA) provide guidelines to protect the rights of culturally diverse students, which demonstrates the critical role of teachers in their academic success.

While our school population continues to become more diverse each year, the teaching force that instructs these students is becoming increasingly white, female, and middle class (Ingersoll & Merrill, 2010; Trent & Artiles, 2007). Teacher preparation programs in general education and special education have not kept pace with the need for more teachers qualified to work effectively with these students (Trent, Kea, & Oh, 2008). Few programs provide the kind of courses and experiences that adequately prepare new teachers to work effectively with English learners; less than one-sixth of pre-service teacher preparation includes training on working with English learners (Ballantyne, Sanderman, & Levy, 2008). While it would be expected that most teachers in U.S. public schools have at least one English learner in the classroom, only 17% of all teachers who work with English learners meet the NCLB requirement of highly qualified teachers (National Center for Education Statistics, 2002). Although 57% of teachers believe they need more training in order to provide effective education

for English learners, only 20 states require that all teachers have such training (Ballantyne, Sanderman, & Levy, 2008). One key factor beyond actual preparation for the job is the way that teachers relate to students. Some teachers have low expectations for English learners and do not establish respectful, supportive relationships with students.

Teacher experience also has an impact on student achievement, with five or more years of teaching considered as the turning point in terms of effectiveness. In 2007, 20% of white 8th graders had teachers with four or fewer years of experience while 30% of Hispanic 8th graders did (Barton & Coley, 2009). Further, schools with high concentrations of English learners are less likely to have fully certified teachers than those with low concentrations of English learners, even after accounting for differences in poverty (Rumburger, Gandara, & Padron, 2006).

All of these factors combine to provide a picture of English learners as disadvantaged, not because of their language, economic status, or cultural differences, but because they have not had the benefit of teachers who have the professional preparation and experience to teach them effectively.

Inappropriate Teaching Practices

The cognitive and linguistic demands of learning content in a second language are tremendous. In classes that do not provide linguistic accommodations, and thus present content as if English learners are native speakers, students don't have access to the curriculum and aren't learning the kind of academic English they need to be successful in school.

In studies that observed classrooms with English learners, instruction tended to be in whole-class settings with students generally doing passive activities, such as watching and listening. Teachers spent more time explaining than questioning, cueing, or prompting students, and they didn't encourage students to extend their oral responses, inadvertently denying them the opportunity to practice using academic English. The lessons were teacher dominated and included few authentic activities or content that related to the students' lives outside of school (Ramirez, et al., 1991; Waxman, Gray, & Padron, 2003).

Further, separating students by ability level for their classes (or by school) continues to be common practice, creating a "poverty of learning" for less advantaged students (Futrell & Gomez, 2008). Studies confirm that minority students and low-income students of all ability levels are overrepresented in the lower tracks and underrepresented in the higher tracks. In our own experience in mostly urban schools, we have witnessed the inequitable situation that research bears out. Segregating English learners from middle-class native English-speaking peers may be particularly harmful because the native language-speaking peers serve as language models, which facilitates English language development (Rumberger, Gandara, & Merino, 2006).

RTI has the potential of ameliorating entrenched practices of tracking students by monitoring each student's progress, changing grouping accordingly, and providing effective instruction, which gives students the enriched learning experiences they need to be successful in school.

At-Risk School Environments

School climate impacts student achievement. Students' perceptions about violence were highly related to their academic achievement (Suarez-Orozco, Suarez-Orozco, & Todorova, 2008). This finding is discouraging given the fact that between 2001 and 2005, Hispanic

students reported an increase in the presence of gangs in schools (38.8% compared to 16.6% of white students) and Hispanic students were more likely to be involved in physical fights (18.3% compared to 11.6% of white students) (Barton & Coley, 2009).

A related topic is that of engagement. In highly volatile environments where students feel at-risk, threatened, or detached from a chaotic school climate, they are less likely to connect with peers, teachers, and staff. The impact on achievement is an interesting one. Positive relationships in school are important for the academic adaptation of students. Relational engagement is strongly correlated with behavioral engagement (students do their best on class work and homework, turn in assignments on time, pay attention and behave appropriately in class, and maintain good attendance), a very important contributor to achievement. Behavioral engagement is highly correlated with grades (Suarez-Orozco, Suarez-Orozco, & Todorova, 2008).

Factors Associated with Educational Success

High Expectations for All Students

Holding high expectations and assuming the best is essential for long-term positive attitudes toward school. Years of research have focused on the self-fulfilling prophesy in the classroom, where teacher expectations affect student achievement and behavior (Brophy & Good, 1970). In our own work, we have seen that when there is a school climate that values students and expects all students to achieve high standards, students outperform similar schools that do not hold high expectations (Echevarria, Short, & Vogt, 2008). The misperception of immigrant students as "pobrecitos" (poor little things) may lead to coddling of nontraditional students, robbing them of challenging learning experiences and achieving success (Adger & Locke, 2000).

High school is a critical time for college preparation or vocational and technical studies, yet in many urban areas, students and staff alike have all but given up on the idea of achieving standards and graduating. Some high schools are beating the odds by offering to all students opportunities that are usually reserved only for the "best" students. Providing a rigorous program of studies along with other features that engage students, these "High Schools That Work" are seeing positive results, which demonstrates the power of high expectations (Bottoms, 2007). In another successful program, even reluctant readers in high-poverty schools eagerly use the critical thinking skills they've learned to discuss, argue, and write about topics, overcoming the misconception that these students "aren't up to" the challenge of a demanding curriculum (Schmoker, 2007).

Effective Teaching Practices

Specific, proven teaching practices are discussed in detail in Chapter 3. In this section we will highlight classroom conditions that lead to achievement. But, it is important to keep in mind that effective instruction for English learners involves the systematic, consistent teaching that the SIOP® Model offers. Picking and choosing favored practices will not lead to the kind of academic achievement our English learners require and deserve.

Overall, highly effective teaching for English learners has a number of characteristics (Kelly, Gomez-Bellenge, Chen, & Schultz, 2008). First, instruction is differentiated for learners so that they are provided with many opportunities to use reading, writing, and

oral language in numerous ways across multiple academic content areas. In addition, teachers scaffold students' literacy attempts so that they will feel free to take risks. Effective teachers respect students' "funds of knowledge" (Moll, et al., 1992) and integrate students' own experiences into lessons, which provides motivation to learn. Finally, use of small group instruction, one-to-one tutoring, extensive reading and cooperative learning also enhances learning for English learners.

Relationships of Respect

School values and expectations are sometimes quite different for English learners than those found in their home; it isn't easy for students from culturally diverse families to adjust to the differing expectations. Foreign-born parents often clash with children's perceptions of the new society's expectations and values. In one study, 80% of immigrant students acknowledged that their parents had different rules than those of American parents (Suarez-Orozco, Suarez-Orozco, & Todorova, 2008).

In her work with ways to help raise achievement for low-income students, Ruby Payne (2008) found that establishing positive relationships with students is a critical factor. She cites actions that show a teacher has respect for students, which were identified by students themselves. They include:

The teacher calls me by my name.

The teacher answers my questions.

The teacher talks to me respectfully.

The teacher notices me and says, "Hi."

The teacher helps me when I need help.

These seemingly simple acts of respect toward students make a huge difference. Further, being conscious of the sociocultural influences on students' lives and the diversity of their life experiences enhances communication and builds positive relationships (Villegas & Lucas, 2007).

RTI and Cultural and Linguistic Diversity

For more than three decades, researchers in bilingual special education have focused on the educational needs of culturally and linguistically diverse populations (Artiles & Trent, 1994; Baca & Cervantes, 1984; Cloud, 1993; Cummins, 1984; Echevarria, 1995; Figueroa, 2002; Gersten, Brengelamn, & Jiminez, 1994; Ortiz & Wilkenson, 1991; Ortiz & Yates, 2002; Rueda, 1989; Ruiz, 1989). As these issues apply to RTI, a cautionary tale unfolds. In addition to the various considerations suggested throughout this book, Jeanette Klinger and colleagues (Klinger & Edwards, 2006; Klinger, Sorrells, & Barrera, 2007) propose that decisions are guided by questions and concerns such as:

- How do we ensure that the child has in fact received culturally responsive, appropriate, quality instruction?
- How do we account for language and culture when designing interventions, conducting research, and generalizing findings?

- What do we mean when we say that instruction or intervention is "evidence-based"? What criteria are applied?

- In considering "evidence-based" interventions, what works with whom, by whom, and in what contexts?

- What does it mean when English learners do not respond to "research-based" instruction?

- To what extent might students be struggling because of limited English proficiency?

- Has adequate support in English language development been provided?

- To what extent has the "research-based" instruction been validated with English learners?

- Are most of the English learners in the classroom succeeding, while just one or two are not? Or are most English learners struggling?

- How should we decide what additional support to provide?

The Important Role of Parents

The importance of parent support is indisputable. Parents' involvement in their child's education is a factor that contributes to student achievement. Parents are also an important support to schools; they create a sense of community between the school and neighborhood, they offer assistance to staff, they are often our best informants about students, and they provide critical insights into cultural attitudes and practices.

Sometimes educators are puzzled when parents of English learners don't participate as fully as expected. Actually, culturally and linguistically diverse parents care very much about their children's success in school and want them to obtain as much education as possible, even through college (Goldenberg, 2006). A study that examined immigrant parent attitudes found that many parents make significant sacrifices in immigrating to the United States, with aspirations of a better life for themselves and their families. Seventy percent of the parents interviewed said that opportunity for their families was the main motivation for immigrating, with 18% explicitly stating that their children's education was the primary reason for coming. Further findings revealed that students themselves value education and recognize the importance of school. The overwhelming majority of students interviewed stated that school prepares you to get ahead and that studying hard leads to success (Suarez-Orozco, Suarez-Orozco, & Todorova, 2008).

Why Don't They Come?

If parents hold such high hopes for their children and communicate to them the value of education, then why is it a common teacher perception that parents are apathetic about their children's education? What are some barriers to active participation by culturally and linguistically diverse parents? The following are some of the many reasons that parents of English learners may not be as fully involved in the school as teachers might expect:

- **Language.** An obvious barrier to participation is not speaking English proficiently. It is likely uncomfortable for parents to be in a situation where they cannot understand the speaker and, in turn, are not understood.

- **Unfamiliarity with the way schools function.** Culturally diverse parents may not understand the importance school personnel place on activities such as back-to-school night, parent-teacher conferences, and open house. Even if they are informed about such activities, they may think it is a courtesy letter and not understand that participation is expected. Further, many culturally diverse parents have responsibilities that preclude their participation, such as work or providing care for elders or young children.

- **Intimidation.** Many parents of English learners have low education levels and often find the level of discourse used and amount of information communicated overwhelming. Further, they may feel that they don't have much to contribute to a discussion with highly educated professionals, particularly in cultures that hold educators in high esteem. Finally, they may have had the common experience of immigrant parents who have been made to feel powerless against the "system."

- **Lack of awareness of their important role.** Parents in general are not familiar with the research on the influence they have on their child's learning; this is especially true with immigrant parents. In many other countries, parents are not encouraged to actively engage in the school and it is the unspoken norm that it is the teacher's job to educate a student (Sobel & Kugler, 2007). Once parents understand their role, they generally become willing participants (Goldenberg, 2004).

- **Economic circumstances.** Most immigrant parents arrive in the new country with very few resources. The poverty rate for children growing up in immigrant homes is double that of native-born families in the United States; they are working poor. Given that, many cannot take time off work to attend meetings and activities.

- **Student's ability/disability.** Having a child who struggles in school because of academic and/or behavior issues can be painful for parents. Conferences that focus almost exclusively on the student's disability and the problems associated with it are a reminder of the dashed hopes and dreams they had for their child. Parents may avoid attending meetings so that they aren't put on the defensive or aren't made to feel like their parenting is being criticized by school personnel. Teachers need to be sensitive about depending on parents to "fix" the student's behavior, motivation, and academic issues because most likely the parents deal with many of the same problems at home – and look to the school for solutions. We want to work in partnership with parents, not overburden them with additional responsibilities. Further, parents respond to having a child with a disability in many different ways. You may know someone whose child struggles academically or socially, yet embraces the attitude that all kids have different strengths and they consider their child's difficulties a part of life. You may know someone else in the same situation who is constantly looking for the right teacher, doctor, or therapist to "cure" the problem. Just as individuals differ in their responses, there are also cultural tendencies. In some cultures, having a disability brings shame on the family, whereas parents from other cultures may consider disability simply a fact of life. School personnel must be aware of cultural attitudes toward disability and, in every case, be extremely sensitive in their interaction with parents of students with disabilities.

What Can We Do?

The characteristics of effective schools include a welcoming attitude toward parents, and formation of connections with the community (Shannon & Bylsma, 2007). We want to

create a school environment that welcomes parent participation as partners, supports their needs, and provides opportunities for family and community involvement. Following are a few suggestions for garnering the support of families of English learners:

- **Be respectful.** School personnel must be welcoming to parents in word and deed. Some front offices in schools are toxic; the staff's attitude is unfriendly at best and sometimes even hostile. Administrators have the responsibility to set a positive, respectful tone in the school that should be reflected by all staff. In particular, parents are affected by the attitude of their child's teacher.

- **Create a sense of community.** With the goal of shared responsibility for the school's success, parents and the school engage in a number of ways. Some schools have sophisticated programs that provide leadership training for immigrant parents, English as a Second Language classes, and parent resource centers (Sobel & Kugler, 2007). If that level of resources isn't available, there are other options for establishing an interdependent relationship between families and schools. Relatively simple yet important events such as weekly Coffee with the Principal communicates to parents that they are an essential partner in the schooling endeavor.

- **Make specific suggestions for helping children academically.** Despite low levels of education, most families have at least one adult or older sibling who can assist children with homework. Also, parents can take their child to the library, look through books and talk about the pictures using the home language, and show enthusiasm for books and reading. In one school where we conducted research, parents attended regularly scheduled after-school "make and take" sessions where they learned, for example, the importance of using flash cards for memorizing math facts and vocabulary words. During the session, parents created a set of materials to use at home.

- **Encourage parent volunteers.** Even parents with low levels of education can have a role in the classroom. They may assist the teacher, volunteer to share an experience or talent (music, cooking, or crafts), and participate in field trips and other events. This kind of participation helps bridge the home-school cultural divide that often exists.

- **Have interpreters available.** Students are often unreliable interpreters because they may screen information (Sobel & Kugler, 2007). Schools should invest in having reliable, trustworthy interpreters on hand to provide information to parents and to assist them in communicating with school personnel. The relationship is most effective when it is two-way, instead of having school personnel unilaterally communicating with parents. Interpreters must be trustworthy because often the information being communicated, especially around the RTI process, is sensitive in nature and needs to remain confidential.

- **Maintain regular communication.** Effective schools regularly send home newsletters that inform parents of what is happening at the school and include resources for parents. The National Center for Learning Disabilities has excellent resources for parents in Spanish to encourage early language and literacy development (http://www.getreadytoread.org/) as do the websites, Colorín Colorado (www.ColorinColorado.org/families), and Reading Rockets (http://www.readingrockets.org/article/18935). In addition to written communication, regular phone calls to report a child's success and home visits are ways to establish good working relationships with families.

Parents and RTI

In effective RTI approaches, parents are informed about their child's progress on a regular basis and their help is enlisted to support the instructional program at home. (See Figure 2.2, A Teacher's Perspective.) In fact, students should also be part of the process; participation by the student creates buy-in that improves the result of intervention (Hosp & Madyun, 2007). The student and parent are provided an opportunity to give their perspective and to discuss whether or not they agree with the school's assessment of areas of difficulty and suggested intervention. Documentation of each participant's input is important (see Figure 2.3) and a contract among the student, teacher, and parent helps ensure maximum results.

FIGURE 2.2 *RTI and Parent Involvement: A Teacher's Perspective*

All parents want their children to succeed in school both academically and socially. However, for many parents involvement in their child's education is a daunting and uncomfortable process. Numerous factors influence this such as: limited understanding of the English language, lack of education, or feelings of intimidation about participating in the school process. Many parents depend on older siblings to navigate the educational path for their younger siblings, which at times is an unrealistic expectation placed upon the sibling.

How can we as educators help parents become more involved with a child who is struggling in school and become active participants in their child's education? For research has time and again shown that a parent's involvement in their child's education is a key factor in that child's success in school.

The Response to Intervention Model (RTI) provides levels of support for students before they begin to fail. The No Child Left Behind Act of 2001 and Individuals with Disabilities Education Improvement Act of 2004 both address the issue of helping students before they fall too far behind in school. With the RTI model educators are now examining a more comprehensive approach to early intervention in the classroom as well as outside of the classroom setting.

One of the key components of RTI in schools across the nation is assisting parents in recognizing the areas where their child is struggling and participating in an integral way in their child's progress in school. Many times parents express concern when the school district wants to "put a label" on their child, for fear that the child will be placed in special education classes and characterized as a child who needs extra assistance throughout his or her education. Without the knowledge behind them, many parents feel intimidated about contacting their child's classroom teacher and approaching the school district for help. They feel frustrated when they see their child failing in school but do not have the necessary expertise to assist the child through the various academic and behavioral supports that are necessary for him or her to succeed.

With the new processes in place using the RTI model, it is important for educators to inform parents in the early stages of a child's education and to be specific about the areas that the child is having difficulty with. They need to provide research-based data to back up their reporting and to inform parents of the interventions that will be employed to assist their child. Educators need to value parent input and realize that most parents really know their child and want to help him or her succeed.

A timetable needs to be clearly defined and parents need to see what the regular education expectation is for that particular skill that is deficient and impeding the child's progress. ... Parents need to be assured that the specific intervention will be done in a timely manner. The district should also provide parents with written material about their data collecting and the various programs being used to help their child improve his or her academic performance.

It would be beneficial for the district to provide parent workshops led by knowledgeable professionals with hands-on training for parents. The workshops could possibly provide parents with specific activities on how they can assist in helping their child succeed at home as well as in the school setting.

On a personal note as an educator I remember a meeting with parents of a special needs student and the parent later told me "I felt like I was at a meeting where no one really cared about my opinion. I felt like everyone was drinking out of ceramic mugs and I was given a Styrofoam cup." Educators need to be aware of the sensitive nature of dealing with both parents and the child who is struggling in school.

FIGURE 2.3 *Parent/Student/Teacher Contract*

K–8 Intensive Intervention Plan: Parent/Student/Teacher Contract

Student's Name _____

Grade: _____   Birth Date: _____

School: _____

Date of Meeting: _____

To be completed by teacher:

1. Basis for determining the academic concern (Circle all that apply):

    ✓ Standards Test

    ✓ Classroom Assessment

    ✓ Report Card Grades

    ✓ Classroom Work Samples

    ✓ Other

2. Language Arts

    ✓ Phonemic Awareness

    ✓ Phonics

    ✓ Reading Comprehension

    ✓ Vocabulary Development

    ✓ Language Development

    ✓ Writing

    ✓ Spelling

3. Mathematics

    ✓ Number Sense

    ✓ Addition

    ✓ Subtraction

    ✓ Multiplication

    ✓ Division

    ✓ Skill Application

    ✓ Other

4. Performance Goal (state expected outcome from intervention):

    _____

    _____

5. Describe the intensive intervention program that would best achieve the performance goal:

    _____

    _____

Completed by: _____

(Continued)

FIGURE 2.3 *Continued*

To be completed by the parent and student:

6. As a parent I agree with the intervention plan and will be responsible for:

- Finding out how my child is progressing by attending conferences, looking at schoolwork, and/or calling the school.

- Providing him/her with a quiet place to study, free of interruption.

- Supervising my child's homework daily.

- Providing at least 20 minutes daily for my child to read silently and/or aloud.

- Providing additional instruction for my child (family member, neighbor, friend, tutor).

- Sending my child to school every day and on time.

- Monitoring the Minder Binder/Student Planner.

- Other plans to assist my child: _____

7. State the dates of implementation: _____

Start Date: _____

Completion Date: _____

I approve the Intensive Intervention Plan for this student:

Teacher's Signature _____

Date _____

Principal/Designee Signature _____

Date _____

I approve the Intensive Intervention Plan for my student:

Parent/Guardian Signature _____

Date _____

I agree with the Intensive Plan, will follow it and will put forth my best effort and cooperation with my teachers and parents.

Student Signature _____

Date _____

Parents should be informed about what progress monitoring is and what it means for their child. (See http://www.studentprogress.org/family/factsheet.asp for family resources and a fact sheet in English and Spanish.) The following questions are important for parents to ask, particularly if their child is being considered for Tier 3 or special education. As mentioned previously, a community worker or other person may be enlisted to assist families in understanding the process and in holding schools accountable. These are modified from questions shown on a website for parents found at http://www.pattan.net/files/RTI/ParentGuide.pdf, slide 4.

1. Is my child's teacher trained in effective instruction for English learners so that I know my child has been provided sufficient opportunities to learn?

2. What research-based programs are being used, and what research supports the effectiveness of the program(s)?

3. Have the programs been validated on culturally and linguistically diverse populations?

4. What process is used to match the intervention(s) to my child's academic, cultural, and linguistic needs?

5. How many weeks and minutes per day of instruction will my child receive in this program?

6. Given my child's English proficiency level, will this amount of time be sufficient?

7. Is a written intervention plan provided to parents in the home language as part of the RTI process?

8. How can parents know that the interventions are being carried out as intended (with fidelity)?

9. What training is required to effectively teach the research-based programs?

10. Is my child's teacher trained in the intervention program as recommended by the publisher?

11. Does training also include issues related to effective teaching for English learners?

Once parents are informed about and understand the importance of high-quality instruction and progress monitoring, some type of communication about the student's performance is sent home regularly. If the student is receiving Tier 2 or Tier 3 intervention, parents need to be informed of the results every couple of weeks (or more frequently) as data are collected and interpreted.

Final Thoughts

Although there has been a long history of underachievement for English learners, the issues discussed in this chapter make it apparent that schools have not always supported culturally and linguistically diverse students in the ways they have needed in order to be successful academically. Some ways schools have failed these students are part of entrenched institutional policies and practices and others are manifested in teacher-student relationships. It is our hope that through effective professional development, educators will learn and implement practices that respect students and their families, and result in effective instructional programs for students. School-wide RTI that emphasizes high-quality instruction for every student holds promise for our English learners.

For Reflection and Discussion

1. The importance of having background knowledge and experiences that align with the content of lessons is undisputed. In your own learning, what are the conditions that facilitate understanding of new concepts or material, and what are impediments to learning?

2. Given the various facts about English learners and their families presented in this chapter, what do you consider to be the greatest impact on teaching and learning?

3. In what ways might you change your approach to working with English learners and their families after reading this chapter?

chapter 3

Tier 1: What Is Best Practice for Teaching English Learners?

The success of the RTI process for culturally and linguistically diverse students depends on teachers having access to appropriate evidence-based instructional approaches that have been validated with diverse populations.

Klinger & Edwards, 2006, p. 113

An Overview of Tier 1: Effective Instruction for English Learners

Tier 1 in RTI is often referred to as the "universal tier" because it is intended to serve the learning needs of all students in the general education classroom. We have known for years that expert teaching based on a high-quality curriculum is effective (Allington & Johnston, 2002; Echevarria, Short, & Powers, 2006; Goldenberg, 2008; Pressley, 2006; Vogt & Shearer, 2011). Embedding research-based, sound practice within RTI exemplifies the interrelatedness between the RTI structure and high-quality instruction. This high-quality, core instruction can be characterized as both preventive and proactive because universal screening instruments and teacher observation provide data about a student's academic and language proficiency. These data guide instructional adjustments and modifications within the regular classroom. For English learners, high-quality instruction requires particular modifications that are especially important if these students are to learn the components of reading, reach grade-level content standards, and develop English proficiency. In this chapter, we review the elements of effective Tier 1 implementation and propose an empirically validated model of Tier 1 instruction, the SIOP® Model, for English learners that includes necessary research-based modifications for effective general education instruction.

For English learners, Tier 1 within RTI includes the following principles:

- It occurs in a general education setting.
- It includes research-based literacy and math (and other) curriculums taught by high-quality teachers who understand the strengths and needs of all students, including English learners.
- Teachers use resources and methods that extend beyond the adopted reading and/or math programs.
- Differentiation aligns assessment and instruction, with flexible grouping for instruction and practice.
- Instruction targets both age-appropriate content concepts and English language development.
- Each student's progress is monitored with reliable, ongoing, and authentic assessments (universal screening), with multiple indicators that are linked explicitly to instruction.

As you read this chapter, refer to Figure 3.1 and think about how you will complete the Guide to Effective RTI Implementation for Tier 1.

In Chapter 1, you contrasted "What is RTI?" and "What is Not RTI?" Similarly, it is important to contrast aspects of what constitutes effective Tier 1 instruction with aspects of more traditional classroom instruction (see Figure 3.2).

FIGURE 3.1 *Guide to Effective RTI Implementation: Tier 1*

Who Is Responsible?	
Necessary Professional Development (For whom and by whom)	
Modification(s) and/or Intervention(s)	
Length of Time	
Teacher-Pupil Ratio	
Assessments Needed	
Assessments Used	
Frequency of Progress Monitoring	
Treatment Fidelity Observation	

(Continued)

FIGURE 3.1 *Continued*

Review of Modification(s) and/or Intervention(s)	
Parent Involvement	
Forms/Resources	

FIGURE 3.2 *Defining Tier 1*

Tier 1 is ...	Tier 1 is not ...
Appropriate, effective, and research-based core instruction for all students (reading, writing, math)	Core instruction in which some students are successful and others are not, and this is perceived as reality
A process that includes formal, universal screening that occurs at least four times a year, focusing on specific skills, strategies, and content knowledge	In-class assessments that focus primarily on what is taught rather than what students know and are able to do
A process that includes formal and informal progress monitoring on an ongoing and continuous basis	Only about determining student progress every nine weeks and at the end of the school year
Instruction with specific adaptations and modifications based on assessment and progress monitoring	One-size-fits-all instruction
Targeted, intense instructional support within the classroom for students who are having difficulty	Reliance on other instructional support staff (e.g., Special Education) to determine a student's needs and to provide remediation
A variety of flexible, grouping configurations for instruction and practice	Whole class instruction, or fixed instructional groups consisting of students who are high, average, and low achievers
A team approach with teachers, administrators, and parents working collaboratively	Teachers who work primarily on their own

Universal Screening in Tier 1

The National Center on Response to Intervention defines screening as follows:

> Screening involves brief assessments that are valid, reliable, and evidence-based. They are conducted with all students or targeted groups of students to identify students who are at risk of academic failure and, therefore, likely to need additional or alternative forms of instruction to supplement the conventional general education approach.
>
> (Retrieved on January 27, 2010 from www.rti4success.org)

Universal screening, a first stage of the RTI screening process, is used to detect or predict students who are or who may be at risk of poor academic outcomes. Instruments used for universal screening are generally brief and all students are assessed with them at each grade level. Additional and more in-depth assessment and/or progress monitoring are necessary to substantiate those students who are identified as being at-risk.

There is a variety of instruments now being used for universal screening in reading and math. It is beyond the scope of this book to list recommended screening instruments because new measures are being created and used regularly, and because they should be selected based upon your students' academic and language needs. However, the National Center on RTI has published a screening tools chart created by the Technical Review Committee (TRC) on Screening. This committee established criteria for evaluating the scientific rigor of screening instruments that were voluntarily submitted for review. The findings of the committee do not constitute endorsement, but they do provide schools and districts with guidance and specific information for selection and use of screening instruments. Additional reading and math screening instruments are added periodically and you are encouraged to check the National Center's website to see what has been added that may be appropriate for your students and educational context. The website is: www.rti4success.org/chart/screeningTools/screeningtoolschart.html. In Tier 1, for both universal screening and follow-up assessments, curriculum-based measurement (CBM) is recommended. CBM enables teachers to learn how students are progressing in the core academic areas. Rather than focusing on mastery, CBM targets increments of growth over time as related to a student's assessed area of need (such as phonemic awareness, oral reading fluency, or medial vowels for beginning readers). With CBM, students are assessed briefly each week for a period of one to five minutes. Results from the brief assessments can be graphed for comparison across a particular interval of time. The value of this type of assessment is the establishment of a baseline (beginning point), checks along the way (performance over time), and determination of an ending point (expected rate of growth). Results from CBM assessments guide teachers in adapting or modifying instruction appropriately. See Chapter 4 for an in-depth discussion of curriculum-based measurement, with specific examples of CBMs that are currently in use in schools and districts.

In addition to CBM screening in the core subjects, it is also possible to screen for student behavior problems. Research-based criteria of risk, such as those provided by DIBELS, are also available when looking at office disciplinary referrals for behavioral issues (see School Wide Information System (SWIS): http://www.swis.org). These criteria can be useful to schools in determining whether students should receive Tier 1, 2, or 3 services.

Progress Monitoring

Another essential element of Tier 1 (as well as the other tiers) is continuous and ongoing progress monitoring. The National Center on Progress Monitoring defines progress monitoring as:

> repeated measurement of academic performance to inform instruction of individual students in general and special education. . . . It is conducted at least monthly to (a) estimate rates of improvement, (b) identify students who are not demonstrating adequate progress and/or (c) compare the efficacy of different forms of instruction to design more effective, individualized instruction.

> (www.rti4success.org)

In RTI, progress monitoring is a scientifically based practice that is used to assess students' academic performance, to quantify a student's rate of improvement or responsiveness to instruction, and evaluate the effectiveness of instruction. Progress monitoring can be implemented with individual students or an entire class. In a nutshell, progress monitoring in Tier 1 involves:

- Data from assessments that guide the monitoring process throughout the period of in-class instruction and intervention;
- A "road map" that provides direction for students' instructional plans;
- The means to adapt and adjust instruction based on assessment data (see Figure 3.3 for a list of possible in-classroom accommodations and/or modifications).

RTI focuses on a problem-solving, collaborative approach that incorporates five stages:

1. **Problem identification:** Based on CBM screening and other assessments, the RTI team (teacher, parents, and administrator or teacher leader) identify specific area(s) of skill deficiency. Based on the screening and other assessment results, the team establishes a baseline or beginning point for instruction.

2. **Problem analysis:** For English learners, this could require analyzing whether the identified problem is an English language proficiency issue or an academic issue. The team sets one or more goals for student progress, and determines an expected rate of growth. See Chapter 2 for more information about important factors.

3. **Implementation of Plan:** Based on screenings, assessment, and teacher observation, a plan is created to overcome the problem within the classroom setting. See Figure 3.3 for an example of a form that can be used to identify and chart classroom adaptations or modifications within Tier 1.

4. **Ongoing assessment/Progress monitoring:** During the targeted time period, the teacher conducts frequent assessment to monitor growth. It is important to use multiple indicators and measures that have been deemed to be reliable and valid for English learners.

5. **Evaluation of Plan:** After a set amount of time (that varies from a few days to a few weeks), the RTI team meets and analyzes the identified student's data from screenings, anecdotal reports, observations, and student work samples. Based on this evaluation, a decision is made about next steps, such as: continuation of the current plan; additional classroom adaptations and/or modifications; more assessment; or a possible move to Tier 2.

FIGURE 3.3 *Classroom Accommodations and/or Modifications*

Classroom Accommodations for English Learners

Student Name _____   Check Accommodations and/or Modifications attempted.

Organization & Management:

- Seat student near teacher
- Stand near student when giving directions/lessons
- Increase distance between desks and peers
- Seat student near positive role model (with L1, if possible, for clarification)
- Avoid distracting stimuli
- Provide peer assistance with organizational skills
- Provide student with extra set of books for home
- Provide student with an assignment notebook
- Provide "how-to" for getting organized
- Check homework daily
- Set and monitor short-term goals for work completion
- Assign volunteer homework buddy (w/same L1, if possible)
- Send daily/weekly progress reports to parents in L1
- Give and model how to do assignments, one at a time
- Give instructions in L1, if possible

Assignments:

- Provide extra time to complete tasks in English
- Simplify complex directions, providing picture support, if needed
- Reduce reading level of assignment, or provide adaptation of text
- Provide visual supports (e.g., photos, illustrations, charts) for texts to be read
- Tape-record reading assignment for homework and/or review
- Divide assignments into shorter segments
- Allow typed assignments (computer)
- Reduce complexity of homework assignments (e.g., partially completed graphic organizers)
- Reduce number of correct responses required (e.g., math problems)
- Provide structured outline in L1 when needed
- Give frequent shorter quizzes; avoid long tests
- Allow use of L1 for expressing knowledge

Lesson Presentation:

- Display and orally review content and language objectives
- Pair students to check work (with L1 peer if needed)
- Write key points and directions on board in clear, neat printing or cursive
- Provide peer tutoring (with L1 peer for clarification)
- Use wide variety of visuals and supplemental materials
- Provide peer note-taker (L1, if needed)
- Make sure directions are understood (model frequently)
- Break longer presentations into shorter segments

Behaviors:

- Provide frequent, immediate, and specific academic feedback
- Model self-monitoring strategies with think-alouds
- Reinforce understanding of classroom expectations in L1, if possible
- Contract with student
- Increase reward immediacy
- Avoid lecturing reprimands
- Use nonverbal cues to stay on task
- Implement classroom behavior system
- Anticipate problems and preventative strategies
- Use meaningful and specific praise related to task accomplishment

(Continued)

Progress Monitoring

FIGURE 3.3 *Continued*

- Provide written outline with simplified language and illustrations
- Allow students to tape-record lesson
- Provide repetition of academic vocabulary
- Have student review key points in L1, if possible
- Teach through multi-sensory modes
- Use computer-aided instruction, as appropriate
- Include meaningful activities for practice and application
- Include final review of all objectives and key vocabulary

- Praise specific behaviors
- Allow legitimate opportunity to move about
- Give rewards and privileges for appropriate behavior
- Implement time-out procedures
- Allow short breaks between assignments
- Ignore minor inappropriate behaviors

Affect:

- Provide reassurance and encouragement
- Speak softly in a non-threatening manner
- Focus on student's talents and accomplishments
- Take time to talk alone with student
- Look for signs of stress build-up and provide encouragement
- Reduce work load temporarily, if needed
- Allow student an opportunity to "save face"
- Provide modeling for anger control
- Encourage student to walk away from conflict
- Compliment positive behavior and work, in L1 if possible (with aide)
- Look for opportunity for student to display leadership role
- Send positive notes home (in L1, if needed)
- Reinforce frequently and specifically when student is frustrated
- Use mild, consistent consequences
- Provide student with choices
- Create a classroom that is respectful of all customs

Test-Taking:

- Allow open book exams
- Give exam orally
- Allow student to give test answers on a tape recorder
- Allow student to use computer to write test answers
- Give frequent short quizzes
- Allow extra time for tests
- Read test item for student (in L1, as needed)
- Give more objective items, fewer essay responses to early-intermediate speakers
- Translate test items into L1, as needed

Things to Consider About Progress Monitoring

1. Carefully choose progress monitoring tools. Curriculum-based measurements (CBM) for English learners must have been normed on populations that include ELs. If possible, select assessments that are available in multiple languages to determine a student's L1 literacy (and math) development. Be careful about over-generalizing, misinterpreting, or over-relying on the findings from any instruments that have not been normed with English learners.

2. Establish a progress monitoring schedule. Assessment schedules vary with each RTI tier and they can be complicated. The instructional intensity for each tier will determine the frequency of assessments. For example, assessments will be given more frequently in Tier 2 than in Tier 1, and more frequently in Tier 3 than in Tier 2.

3. Interpret the results of progress monitoring. This is perhaps the most challenging aspect of RTI. Consider graphing data to provide a visual representation of baseline, target line (expected growth), and trend line data (performance over time). Again, multiple and multi-dimensional indicators provide the best picture of student growth and achievement. For example, to gain a full understanding of a young child's literacy development, a teacher might collect reading data on his or her letter recognition, oral and silent reading comprehension, phonemic awareness, phonics, and other decoding skills (e.g., use of context). Multi-dimensionality means that the child's writing development (e.g., use of invented spelling, syntax, and vocabulary knowledge), and oral language development would also be assessed.

In reality, for many teachers, the RTI screenings, other assessments, progress monitoring, record keeping, and planning and teaching of lessons can be daunting. It's also difficult to examine your own teaching with insight when you're just trying to keep a lid on things in the everyday running of a classroom. Therefore, it is imperative in Tier 1 that a collaborative approach is taken with each RTI step and process. The old notion of "my kids" in "my classroom" no longer exists within RTI. *All* students are *everyone's* concern, and all successes are the result of an effective, supportive, and collaborative RTI process and effort.

Many districts are organizing collaborative efforts around progress monitoring and instructional decisions based on data results. In one large urban district, teams consisting of the school psychologist, social worker, special education teacher, principal, and grade level teachers meet at least three times a year with each grade level to discuss progress monitoring data. Figure 3.4 shows an example of the kind of tracking chart that can be used at a glance to identify those students who need intervention and then it monitors their progress across time.

Challenges in Tier 1 Universal Screening and Progress Monitoring for English Learners

There are several considerations for Tier 1 screening and progress monitoring for English learners. These are important to keep in mind when using screening and diagnostic instruments written in English. For example, what might appear to be a student's "error," could

FIGURE 3.4 *Winter Data Analysis Grades 3–5*

MAP TIERS: Tier 3: 0-10th %ile, Tier 2: 11th-32nd %ile, Tier 1: 33rd-66th %ile, Tier 1+: 67th %ile+*AIMSweb R-CBM (fluency) TIERS:* Tier 3: 0-10th %ile, Tier 2: 11th-24th %ile, Tier 1: 25th-75th %ile, Tier 1+: 76th %ile+*IDEL TIERS:* Tier 3: At Risk/medium gray, Tier 2: Some Risk/light gray, Tier 1: Low-Risk/dark gray

Student Name	Winter MAP *Total* RIT	Winter MAP Tier	+/– Fall MAP *Total* RIT	AIMSweb Winter R-CBM	AIMSweb Winter Tier	+/– Fall AIMSweb R–CBM	IDEL Winter FLO	IDEL Winter Tier	+/– Fall IDEL FLO
	160	1%/3	+7	20/45	T3	+25	27/45	T3	+18
	161	1%/3	+7	26/50	T2	+24	39/60	T2	+21
	162	1%/3	+10	24/22	T3	–2	38/50	T3	+12
	164	1%/3	+4	40/89	T1	+49	62/65	T2	+3
	171	4%/3	+11	71/91	T1	+20	74/92	T1	+18
	172	4%/3	+20	41/57	T2	+16	55/70	T1	+15
	173	5%/3	0	47/52	T2	+5	46/66	T2	+20
	176	8%/3	+19	72/100	T1	+28	89/104	T+1	+15
	176	8%/3	+20	39/49	T3	+10	51/72	T1	+21
	178	10%/3	0	53/81	T1	+28	60/65	T2	+5
	178	10%/3	+14	43/69	T2	+26	61/74	T1	+13
	181	14%/2	+14	78/127	T+1	+49	91/104	T+1	+13
	181	14%/2	+24	41/44	T3	+3	43/65	T2	+22
	185	21%/2	–4	90/99	T1	+9	85/91	T1	+6
	191	34%/1	+16	48/60	T2	+12	69/81	T1	+12
	198	54%/1	+12	97/108	T1	+11	69/75	T1	+12
	198	54%/1	+13	68/98	T1	+26	78/88	T1	+10
	202	65%/1	+5	77/106	T1	+29	88/112	T+1	+24
	202	65%/1	–3	155/156	T+1	+1	112/125	T+1	+13
	205	74%/1	+5	102/120	T+1	+18	101/107	T+1	+6
	213	91%/1	–1	129/136	T+1	+7	113/116	T+1	+3

Developed by Laura Gonzalez Coloccia, School Psychologist

instead be confusion about English or a generalization the student is making from his or her home language to English. Therefore, consider the following as you are assessing, planning, and monitoring Tier 1 teaching within RTI (Echevarria, Vogt, & Short, 2008; Echevarria, Vogt, & Short, 2010a; Echevarria, Vogt, & Short, 2010b):

- English learners need explicit instruction in the aspects of English that may differ from their native languages (L1), including the phonology, morphology, and syntax of English. Without explicit teaching, a student's results on a screening instrument may be skewed because, for example, some phonemes of English do not exist in some other languages. Likewise, some phonemes in other languages do not exist in English. If this is the case, a youngster may not be able to correctly recognize or produce the sound of a phoneme that is being tested without a great deal of practice. A wonderful resource that includes a systematic spelling and phonics inventory in Spanish, Chinese, and Korean is *Words Their Way for English Learners: Word Study for Phonics, Vocabulary, and Spelling Instruction* (Bear, Helman, Templeton, Invernizzi, & Johnston, 2007). Word lists that can be used for word identification and sorting activities are included in English, Spanish, Arabic, Chinese, Korean, and Vietnamese.

- Many Latin and Greek roots in English are also found in the morphemes of other languages. For example, for students whose L1 is Spanish, there are many cognates that link English vocabulary and spellings with Spanish words (*estudier* = study; *excepción* = exception). Cognates are also found in French/English, German/English, and other morphologically based languages. For other examples, along with suggestions for how to teach cognates, see Vogt and Echevarria (2008).

- Determining overall reading proficiency in English for English learners can be challenging and sometimes misleading. It is important first to assess a student's reading proficiency in the home language, if possible. Students who are readers in their L1 can transfer their knowledge of the reading process to English, which, of course, is an easier task than learning to read in a new language. Readers whose first language is non-alphabetic can transfer comprehension strategies to English; they will, of course, need to learn a new alphabetic sound-symbol system in order to read, write, speak, and understand English.

- Other English learners may have underdeveloped or nonexistent literacy skills in either their first language or English. We know that the five sub-components of reading instruction as identified by the National Reading Panel (2000)—phonemic awareness, phonics, fluency, vocabulary, and comprehension—are the same sub-components we must focus on when teaching English learners (August & Shanahan, 2008). So, rather than immediately referring these youngsters for special help, first we must provide explicit, high-quality instruction in each of the sub-components, with regular assessment and purposeful progress monitoring. For additional information about English language literacy development, see *Developing Reading and Writing in Second-Language Learners* (August & Shanahan, 2008), and *Effective Literacy and English Language Instruction for English Learners in the Elementary Grades* (Gersten, Baker, Shanahan, Linan-Thompson, Collins, & Scarcella, 2007).

- Be careful about using some types of comprehension assessments found in commercial reading programs to estimate students' reading levels. These sometimes require that a student silently and orally read a grade-level passage, while the teacher notes the student's fluency (correct words per minute), vocabulary recognition, and comprehension (via questions at the end of the reading activity). An English learner (depending on level of English proficiency) is at a decided disadvantage with this type of

assessment, especially when it consists of timed readings. Be very careful about over-generalizing results from these leveled reading inventories, especially if they have not been normed with English learners, and if possible, try to establish a reading level in the student's home language prior to administering an assessment of this kind. Jerry Johns's *Basic Reading Inventory* (2008) includes a Spanish version of the Inventory for grades K–4 (normed with English learners) with vocabulary and comprehension assessments that would be helpful for Spanish-speaking children and adolescents.

- Remember that successful reading of any text is also dependent on other variables, including familiarity with the topic being read, vocabulary knowledge, the flexible use of a variety of reading skills and strategies, motivation, and purpose setting. Our usual battery of reading assessments may not yield reliable results for English learners, and selection of appropriate texts is considerably more difficult. A student assessed at grade level in a native language text may be assessed at a considerably lower level when reading English, so caution is advised about assigning a "reading level" from an Informal Reading Inventory in English, without other pertinent assessment information.

- The National Center on Student Progress Monitoring (www.rti4success.org) has on its website a review of progress monitoring tools that you might find to be helpful.

High-Quality Classroom Instruction Making Content Comprehensible for English Learners: The SIOP® Model

"Because teaching is complex, it is helpful to have a road map through the territory, structured around a shared understanding of teaching colleagues" (Danielson, 2007).

The SIOP® Model (Echevarria, Vogt, & Short, 2008; 2010a; 2010b) was designed and researched extensively to help classroom teachers systematically, consistently, and concurrently teach grade-level academic content and academic language to English learners. The SIOP® Model is effective with both English learners and native English-speaking students who are still developing academic literacy (Echevarria, Short, & Powers, 2006; Short, Fidelman, & Louguit, 2009).

The SIOP® Model consists of eight components and thirty features that when implemented to a high degree, have positively impacted the academic achievement and English language development for English learners (see Appendix A for the complete SIOP® protocol). The SIOP® Model is an instructional framework for organizing classroom instruction in meaningful and effective ways—and may be used across all Tiers (see example in Chapter 1). Although the SIOP® Model is now effectively implemented in bilingual, ESL, and two-way immersion classrooms, it is primarily intended as a model of sheltered instruction for all content classrooms (pre-K–12) where the language of instruction is English. The SIOP® Model is now being implemented in all fifty states as well in numerous countries, and it represents the best hope for high-quality Tier 1 instruction for English learners.

The following overview briefly describes each of the SIOP® components, followed by research and citations culled from several recent research syntheses on English learner language acquisition and literacy. In Chapter 1, we introduced an RTI framework that includes high-quality classroom instruction with the SIOP Model as ideal Tier 1 teaching

for English learners (see Figure 1.2). If you are unfamiliar with the SIOP® Model, it is critically important that you read one of the core SIOP® texts (Echevarria, Vogt, & Short, 2008; 2010a; or 2010b) before you look to the Model for Tier 1 instruction. Our research findings clearly indicate that fidelity to the SIOP® Model is imperative if English learners' academic and language proficiency is to be increased significantly. Reading the core text and using the SIOP® protocol for lesson planning, observations, and discussion results in higher levels of SIOP® implementation (see Appendix A: SIOP® protocol).

Components of the SIOP® Model

Lesson Preparation

The focus for each SIOP® lesson is content and language objectives that are clearly defined, displayed, and orally reviewed with students. These objectives are linked to content standards and the academic vocabulary and language that students need for success. For teachers, the goal is to help students gain important experience with key grade-level content and skills as they progress toward fluency in English. Students know what they are expected to learn and/or be able to do by the end of each lesson. They have a road map at the start of each lesson so that they can focus on what is important and take an active part in the learning process. Also within this component, teachers provide supplementary materials (e.g., visuals, multimedia, adapted or bilingual texts, publisher-supplied summaries of literature selections, and study guides) because grade-level reading and math series may be difficult for many English learners to comprehend. Adaptations are provided through special texts, supportive handouts, and audio-taped selections such as often come with reading series, and texts appropriate for varied English proficiency levels. Graphic organizers and illustrations are used for pre-reading activities and for teaching key points. Also, meaningful activities provide access to the key concepts in the English-language arts or math lessons, and provide opportunities for students to apply their content and language knowledge.

Research Support for the Lesson Preparation Component

- English learners benefit from ELD (English Language Development) instruction, but they also need instruction in the use of English in the content areas. Teaching both content and language is a challenge for teachers (Lyster, 2007).

- "As a general rule, all students tend to benefit from clear goals and learning objectives . . ." (Goldenberg, 2008, p. 17).

- An important theme in studies that investigated English learner literacy instruction is that of attending to students' individual needs, since English learners are not a homogeneous group. English learners need a variety of activities and instructional materials in varied settings (August, et al., 2008) that are geared to their experiential and educational backgrounds, and their levels of English language proficiency (Echevarria, Short, & Powers, 2006).

- When planning lessons for English learners, teachers must understand the context in which they develop as readers. The attributes a student brings to school (such as

knowledge, beliefs, attitudes, motivations, behaviors, experiences with specific contexts and situations) impact how he or she deals with school. "The greater the differences in these attributes and the school experiences, the greater the hindrance to learning" (Goldenberg, Rueda, & August, 2008, p. 105).

Building Background

In SIOP® lessons, teachers connect new concepts with students' personal experiences and past learning. Teachers build background knowledge because many English learners have not attended U.S. schools or are unfamiliar with American culture. At other times, it's necessary to activate students' prior knowledge in order to learn what students already know, to identify misinformation, or to discover when it's necessary to fill in gaps. English learners may have funds of knowledge different from native English speakers and teachers can tap them as resources, perhaps in lessons related to short story characters or plots, poetry, native-language nursery rhymes, songs they have learned previously, universal themes in literature, and so forth. As teachers prepare lessons, they can examine the anthologies, novels, and other texts used for cultural biases or idiomatic speech so potential problems can be anticipated, or potentially confusing concepts can be pre-taught. Granted, idiomatic expressions are generally taught as part of the language arts curriculum, but for English learners, teachers need to be especially sensitive to figurative language that may pop up in conversations, literature, and informational texts.

The SIOP® Model places great significance on building a broad vocabulary base for students. We need to pay more attention to vocabulary instruction across the curriculum so students become effective readers, writers, speakers, and listeners. Most language arts teachers explicitly teach key vocabulary and word structures, word families, and word relationships. Go further for English learners by helping them develop word learning strategies beyond decoding. Share strategies such as using context clues, word parts (i.e., affixes), visual aids (e.g., illustrations), and cognates (a word related in meaning and form to a word in another language). Design lesson activities that give students multiple opportunities to use new vocabulary both orally and in writing. In order to move words from receptive knowledge to expressive use, vocabulary needs reinforcement through different learning modes.

Research Support for the Building Background Component

- Studies of vocabulary instruction show that ELs learn more words through explicit instruction; by working with words that are embedded in meaningful contexts; by having many opportunities for repetition and use of the words in reading, writing, listening, and speaking; when the words are posted and reviewed; and when they are working with words in multiple texts and contexts (Beck, McKeown, & Kucan, 2002; Carlo, et al., 2004).

- "A small but consistent body of intervention research suggests that English learners will benefit most from rich, intensive vocabulary instruction that emphasizes 'student-friendly' definitions, that engages students in meaningful use of word meanings in reading, writing, speaking, and listening, and that provides regular review" (Gersten, et al., 2007).

● Teachers can help English learners by having students read about topics with which they have some familiarity, and by making sure students have adequate exposure to the topic prior to reading about it (Jiménez, Garcia, & Pearson, 1996).

Comprehensible Input

If information is presented in a way that students cannot understand, such as an explanation that is spoken too rapidly, or reading selections that are far above students' reading levels with no visuals or graphic organizers to assist them, many students—including English learners—will be unable to learn the necessary content. Instead, modify "traditional" instruction with a variety of ESL methods and SIOP® techniques so students are able to comprehend the lesson's key concepts. Examples of these techniques are:

● Teacher talk that is appropriate to student proficiency levels;

● Demonstrations and modeling of tasks, processes, and routines;

● Gestures, pantomime, and movement to make concepts more clear;

● Opportunities for students to engage in role-plays, improvisation, and simulations;

● Visuals and supplementary materials, such as pictures, real objects, illustrations, charts, adapted texts, audiotapes or CDs, perhaps in the native language, if needed and available;

● Restatement, paraphrasing, repetition, and written records of key points;

● Previews and reviews of important information;

● Hands-on, experiential, and discovery activities.

Remember that academic tasks must be explained clearly and in steps, both orally and in writing for students. We cannot assume English learners know how to do an assignment because it is a regular routine for the rest of your students. Talk through the procedures and use models and examples of good products and appropriate participation, so students know the steps they should take and can envision the desired result.

Research Support for the Comprehensible Input Component

● For beginning English speakers, "teachers will have to speak slowly and somewhat deliberately, with clear vocabulary and diction, and use pictures, other objects, and movements to illustrate the content being taught" (Goldenberg, 2008, p. 23).

● Reducing the complexity of language is effective when used judiciously. Oversimplification of spoken and written language limits exposure to varied sentence constructions and language forms (Crossley, McCarthy, Louwerse, & McNamara, 2007).

● Visual representations, not just language-based explanations, provide students with needed, additional support (Scarcella, 2003).

Strategies

This SIOP® component addresses student learning strategies, teacher-scaffolded instruction, and higher-order thinking skills. By explicitly teaching cognitive and metacognitive learning strategies, teachers equip students for academic learning both inside and outside

the SIOP® classroom. Capitalize on the learning strategies students already use in their first language because those can transfer to the new language.

SIOP® teachers frequently scaffold instruction so students can be successful with academic tasks. Support efforts at their current performance level but also move English learners to a higher level of understanding and accomplishment. When they master a skill or task, remove the supports that were provided and add new ones for the next level. The goal, of course, is the gradual release of responsibility so that English learners can achieve independence one step at a time.

Teachers need to remember to ask English learners a range of questions, some of which should require critical thinking. It is easy to ask simple, factual questions, and sometimes we fall into that trap with students acquiring English, but we must go beyond questions that can be answered with a one- or two-word response. Instead, ask questions and create projects or tasks that require students to think more critically and to apply their language skills in a more extended way. Remember an important adage: "Just because ELs don't speak English proficiently, doesn't mean they can't *think*."

Research Support for the Strategies Component

- The CREDE report (Genesee, Lindholm-Leary, Saunders, & Christian, 2006) suggests that instruction for English learners should combine both direct and interactive approaches. This includes a give-and-take between teacher and students, and also a teacher who encourages higher levels of thinking, speaking, and reading.

- Three types of learning strategies that have been identified in the research literature include metacognitive strategies, cognitive strategies, and social/affective strategies (O'Malley & Chamot, 1990).

- Students benefit from receiving explicit instruction in how to use a variety of learning strategies flexibly and in combination (Dole, Duffy, Roehler, & Pearson, 1991).

- Teaching learning strategies has a long history of research supporting its efficacy (Echevarria & Graves, 2010; Vaughn, Gersten, & Chard, 2000).

- "One issue that emerges from . . . studies has to do with strategy use versus teacher's scaffolding of text as a mechanism for improving students' comprehension. For example, [the teacher] presumably focused on teaching students strategy use. However, [he] did many things that scaffolded instruction. . . . Future studies on strategy use would benefit from clearly distinguishing the two methods of building comprehension . . ." (August, et al., 2008, p. 153).

Interaction

We know that students learn through interaction with one another and with their teachers. They need oral language practice to help develop and deepen their content knowledge and support their second language reading and writing skills. Clearly, the teacher is the main role model for appropriate English usage, word choice, intonation, fluency, and so forth, but do not discount the value of student-student interaction. In pairs and in small groups, English learners practice new language structures and vocabulary that they have been taught as well as important language functions, such as asking for clarification, confirming interpretations, elaborating on one's own or another's idea, and evaluating opinions.

Sometimes the interaction patterns expected in an American classroom differ from students' cultural norms and prior schooling experiences. We need to be sensitive to sociocultural differences and work with students to become competent in the culture that has been established in the classroom, while respecting students' values, backgrounds, languages, and cultures.

Research Support for the Interaction Component

- Second-language learning is a social process: Language develops largely as a result of meaningful interaction with others, much as a first language does (Saunders & Goldenberg, in press).

- Structured interaction between ELs and native English (EO) speakers does not result in proficiency gains when it focuses primarily on "supportive and friendly discourse." Language proficiency gains were found when the EL-EO interactions focused more on negotiation of meaning or efforts to elicit "comprehensible input" (Foster & Ohta, 2005, as reported in Saunders & Goldenberg, in press).

- Promising practices for improving English learners' comprehension include cooperative learning and discussion, such as instructional conversations (August & Shanahan, 2008).

- Interactive activities that effectively mix English learners and more proficient English learners or native speakers of English typically involve carefully structured tasks. The overall finding is that treatments with interactive tasks produced a significant and substantial effect on language learning outcomes (Saunders & Goldenberg, in press).

- Oral language proficiency impacts all aspects of educational achievement: higher grades and achievement test results (August & Shanahan, 2006; Suarez-Orozco, et al., 2008); and the acquisition of skilled reading (Lesaux & Giva, 2008).

- Interaction is important for developing friendships, which are important for immigrant English learners (Suarez-Orozco, et al., 2008).

- "Probably the most obvious instructional modification is to use the primary language for clarification and explanation. This can be done by the teacher, a classroom aide, a peer, or a volunteer in the classroom" (Goldenberg, 2008, p. 19).

- "[T]eaching English vocabulary is effective, but progress may be most rapid when this instruction is connected to the students' home language, such as by providing a home-language equivalent or synonym for new words or focusing on shared cognates when available" (August, et al., 2008).

Practice & Application

Practice and application of new material is important for all learners. Research on the SIOP® Model found that lessons with hands-on, visual, and other kinesthetic tasks benefit ELs because students practice the language and content knowledge through multiple modalities. SIOP® teachers ensure that lessons include a variety of activities that encourage students to apply both the content and language skills they are learning. For English learners to learn the language, it is imperative that they practice and apply literacy and language processes (reading, writing, listening, speaking) in every lesson.

Research Support for the Practice & Application Component

- It is well established that practice and application helps one master a skill (Jensen, 2005; Marzano, Pickering, & Pollock, 2001).

- For English learners at risk for reading problems, teachers should provide intensive small-group reading interventions in which students have multiple opportunities to practice reading words and sentences (Gersten, et al., 2007).

- Students benefit from opportunities to practice, apply, and transfer new learning (Goldenberg, 2008).

Lesson Delivery

This component focuses on determining if the delivery of a lesson supports the content and language objectives. Further, throughout the lesson in a SIOP® classroom, the majority of students are highly engaged. We know that lesson preparation is crucial to effective delivery, but so are classroom management skills. SIOP® teachers have clear routines to follow, they make sure students know the lesson's content and language objectives so everyone stays on track, they introduce (and revisit) meaningful activities that appeal to students, they provide appropriate wait time so English learners can process concepts, and the classroom instruction fosters high student engagement. A lesson shouldn't move either too slowly or too quickly; student comprehension of key concepts is the goal so teachers monitor comprehension carefully throughout each lesson.

Research Support for the Lesson Delivery Component

- English learners need much richer and more extensive teaching procedures than are usually recommended in core curricular programs (August, Carlo, Dressler, & Snow, 2005; Blachowicz, Fisher, Ogle, & Watts-Taffe, 2006).

- Students benefit from "well-designed, clearly structured, and appropriately paced instruction; active engagement and participation . . . this is as likely to be true for English learners as it is for English speakers" (Goldenberg, 2008, p. 17).

Review & Assessment

Each SIOP® lesson needs time for review and assessment. Teachers do English learners a disservice if they spend the last five minutes teaching a new concept rather than reviewing what students have learned so far. Therefore, SIOP® teachers revisit key vocabulary and concepts with students throughout the lesson and as a final wrap-up. They check on student comprehension frequently throughout the lesson period to determine whether additional explanations or re-teaching are needed. During formative and summative assessment, be sure to provide multiple and differentiated indicators for students to demonstrate their understanding of the content and language instruction.

Research Support for the Review & Assessment Component

- At-risk English learners benefit from clear feedback from the teacher when students make errors (Gersten, et al., 2007).

- Students benefit from feedback on correct and incorrect responses, periodic review and practice, frequent assessments to gauge progress, and re-teaching when needed (August & Shanahan, 2008).

- "Data from screening and progress monitoring assessments should be used to make decisions about the instructional support English learners need to learn to read" (Gersten, et al., 2007, p. 3).

Uses and Benefits of the SIOP® Model

While for purposes of RTI, we are suggesting that the SIOP® Model represents high-quality Tier 1 teaching for all students, it is also being successfully introduced in pre-service teacher preparation programs. The SIOP® framework brings needed coherence to teacher preparation programs when new teachers are learning how to teach English learners (Vogt, 2009). Rather than viewing each content methods course as a separate entity, the SIOP® Model brings together all content classes in a systematic framework for effective classroom instruction.

Once in the classroom (pre-K–12), novice teachers are able to organize their teaching when the SIOP® protocol (see Appendix A) is used for lesson planning, curriculum discussions, and observations with conferencing. For example, Lela Alston Elementary School in Isaac School District, Phoenix, AZ, a school in which all teachers have had extensive SIOP® training, provides immediate SIOP® professional development and SIOP® mentors for all teachers who are new to the school (Echevarria, Short, & Vogt, 2008). It is very important to recognize and remember that the SIOP® protocol is not an instrument intended to be used for teacher *evaluation*. Instead, SIOP® lessons are observed and rated to determine the degree of implementation of each of the SIOP® features.

Experienced teachers have found that the SIOP® Model has enhanced and refined their teaching practices through purposeful and principled decision-making that is based on assessment of students' strengths and needs (Echevarria, Short, & Vogt, 2008, p. 175). The principal of Lela Alston Elementary School, Debbie Hutson, states:

> Improvement has been seen . . . with them [the teachers] teaching more. I mean, like up on their feet teaching more and working really hard to keep students engaged. I think their planning is much more effective. I think, too, with all of the training and all the different components that we've done, the teachers are so much more aware.

We have seen average teachers become very good teachers, and very good teachers become excellent teachers when they implement the SIOP® Model. There is no question that substantive professional development coupled with study of the core SIOP® text (Echevarria, Vogt, & Short, 2008; 2010a; 2010b) is essential if teachers are to become high-implementing SIOP® teachers.

One of the advantages of the SIOP® Model for Tier 1 classroom instruction is that it provides a common language for instruction. In our work with educators who were

committed to building wide reform and best practice, the common language that the SIOP® Model provides has often been cited as an important factor in a school's success (Echevarria, Short, & Vogt, 2008).

Differentiated Instruction

Most teachers agree that it is important to differentiate instruction to meet the academic needs of all students. However, making this happen on a consistent, systematic basis is considered by many to be next to impossible, especially when a classroom consists of academically, linguistically, and culturally diverse students. High-implementing SIOP® teachers have found that they differentiate their instruction frequently and naturally when they incorporate consistently the thirty features of the SIOP® Model in their lessons. SIOP® teachers adapt and modify instructional materials and practices for English learners and other students. Appropriate differentiation does not imply that equality equates to fairness, or that fairness equates to equality (Diller, 2007), because what works for one student may not work or be appropriate for others. Within RTI, the goal is to provide the best instruction possible given a student's assessed needs. Therefore, differentiation can occur in the classroom in many ways through diverse content, processes, and products (Tomlinson, 1999), as long as assessment data and content and language objectives guide the way.

As you read the following "In Her Own Words," think about the suggestion that Ms. Nash makes regarding the powerful effects of relatively simple classroom differentiation. By asking Marco to identify his concerns, the principal was able to assist his teacher in creating a learning environment more suitable to his needs. Sometimes teachers think that differentiation is complex and complicated, but in reality, sometimes small adaptations can make the biggest difference for a child.

In Her Own Words: A Principal's Classroom Observation

by Mardell Nash
Los Alamitos Unified School District, CA

This past summer I had the opportunity to observe a classroom with a group of students in the fifth grade with a wide range of abilities, but who were all performing well below grade level and were recommended to summer school for a four-week intensive intervention program. Some of the students were there to work on their comprehension skills and others attended to work on decoding and mathematical skills.

Of particular concern in one classroom that I visited was a student, Marco, who was constantly being referred to the office because he was distracting other students and was unable to finish his work. Marco continually got up and walked around the classroom to get a drink, sharpen his pencil or get a tissue. When the teacher checked with him, he had only begun the assignment, while over half of the class had already completed the work.

I had Marco accompany me to the office and asked him what the problem was. His first response was that he was hungry and hadn't eaten any breakfast that morning. However, when I continued the line of questioning, Marco said that the classroom was too

noisy for him to concentrate on his work. He specifically pointed out two students who sat by him and who were constantly talking. I then asked Marco if he could list some of the things that made learning difficult for him. I told him I would write the things down on a piece of paper and he could list them for me. Here is the list of things Marco stated that made the classroom assignments hard for him:

1. *The noise level of other students, especially ones who were sitting near him;*
2. *He was unsure of how to organize his work and decide on what he should do first;*
3. *Sometimes when he was reading he wasn't sure about the meaning of certain words;*
4. *He didn't think he was very good at the task and didn't find it fun or engaging.*

We then took the list and brainstormed together solutions to help Marco be more successful in the classroom. I explained that he needed to take responsibility for his learning but that I would assist him in making the tasks less challenging. We looked over his assignments, decided which one was the most important, and how we'd attack it before moving on to the next. We talked about the importance of completing one assignment before beginning another one. We also talked about putting his assignments on his desk in the order they are to be completed. I suggested that Marco keep a piece of paper by his desk and write down any words that he was unsure of when reading, and to show the teacher those words so she could explain them at an appropriate time. I asked the teacher if Marco could present the word list to her each day and if they could create a list of words that Marco could practice at home.

When examining his classroom, I discussed with the teacher a more suitable, far less distracting place for Marco to sit. I also asked her to pair Marco with a peer whose reading level was somewhat higher than his own. I suggested that when they read together, each student read one sentence at a time, alternating between sentences, thus requiring both students to attend to the print. When I checked back with Marco and the teacher later on in the day, the teacher was impressed with Marco's ability to focus on his task and the amount of disruptions were greatly reduced.

The simple accommodations described here are easy and effective techniques for any classroom teacher to use. At the end of the four-week period, Marco was experiencing success. He was completing his classroom assignments in an appropriate length of time and was not disruptive to his peers in the classroom.

A Glimpse into a Classroom with High-Quality Instruction for English Learners

To illustrate one way to make instruction meaningful for English learners, a writing process is described and student work samples are included to demonstrate the results of interesting, engaging writing lessons, as seen in Appendix C. From a classroom in Texas, Title 1 Specialist Vicki Roberts shares a process that she and Lina Nino used throughout the year in Ms. Nino's grade 4 class, where Ms. Roberts worked each Wednesday. In Shorehaven Elementary School, 80% of the students are economically disadvantaged; 37.7% are designated as Limited English Proficient (LEP), and 58.9% are categorized as At Risk.

On the district writing test this year, 56% of the students in Ms. Nino's class were commended on the writing test, meaning that on the written composition they had to receive a score of 3 or 4 on their writing on a 4-point scale. In contrast, in the population of all students tested in the district, 34% were commended. Comparing the total LEP population in the district, they had a commended rate of 19%. This was the first year the students were tested in writing, so there are no comparison scores for this group. As you read about the process in Appendix B, think about what these educators did to enable their English learners to become successful writers.

Final Thoughts

For too many years, when English learners have been unsuccessful learning to read, write, or do math, they have been referred to and placed in special education programs. At the same time, other English learners who perhaps needed special education services were not appropriately placed because of the difficulties in assessing the difference between a learning "problem" and a language "proficiency" issue. Common sense and data suggest that the percentage of ELs in special education should be equal to the percentage of students representing all other demographics. However, that has not been the case, in large part, because classroom instruction for English learners has been ineffective for this population of students.

The SIOP® Model has been found to be a reliable, valid, and empirically sound framework for teaching English learners (and others) in the mainstream classroom. At the heart of high-quality instruction for ELs is appropriate assessment that accurately identifies their unique language and academic strengths and needs. Effective Tier 1 instruction within RTI for English learners is exemplified through the SIOP® Model with the type of differentiated instruction described in the classroom stories within this chapter. We hope that you will consider the SIOP® Model for exemplary Tier 1 instruction within RTI and that your students and teachers both benefit greatly from implementing the Model.

For Reflection and Discussion

1. Tier 1 instruction requires that teachers provide high-quality, effective instruction for all students that is based on assessment, content standards, and regular monitoring of student progress. As you think about the professional development that will be required to bring this about, who are the key players (both faculty and administrators) who need to take leadership in this endeavor? What will be each of their responsibilities, and what is a reasonable timeline for putting the RTI pieces in place? What are some possible pitfalls? What are your collective, expected goals for determining success in Tier 1? Turn to Appendix D and select one of the three profiles, answer the questions, and discuss your responses with your RTI team members.

2. Becoming a high-implementing SIOP® teacher is also a process that requires professional development, planning, and time. Reflect on your answers to the questions in the preceding exercise. In what ways can SIOP® professional development intersect with Tier 1 planning and your overall RTI goals? This intersection is critically important for English learners, but what might be some advantages for native speakers whose academic achievement and language proficiency are lacking?

Tier 2 Interventions for English Learners

By Catherine Richards-Tutor

Focused classroom [instruction] is not sufficient to meet the needs of some children. To accelerate their progress and ensure that they do not slip further behind, these students require more strategic intervention . . .

Vaughn, Wanzek, Woodruff, & Linan-Thompson, 2007

FIGURE 4.1 *Defining Tier 2*

Tier 2 is...	Tier 2 is NOT....
Supplemental instruction.	A replacement of core curriculum (if students are not getting the core program, they will only fall further behind).
Focused and targeted on specific skills that are associated with broader academic successes.	Time to reteach a standard(s) that students did not master such as changing decimals and percents in math or character traits in language arts. (This reteaching needs to be done in Tier 1.)
Designed for students who are not making adequate progress on core skills that are associated with broader academic success.	Designed for students who did not master a standard. (These students need to receive differentiated instruction in Tier 1; see Chapter 3.)
Explicit instruction that emphasizes key instructional features we know to be important for English learners: opportunities for developing and practicing oral language, key vocabulary emphasis, interaction, learning strategy instruction, etc.	A replacement for English Language Development (ELD).
For approximately 20–25% of the students in a given class, grade level, or school.	For more than 30% of the students in a given class, grade level, or school (if it is the case that more than 30% of the students need Tier 2 interventions, it is time to rethink Tier 1—what can we do to improve this level of instruction?

For some English learners, Tier 1 instruction might not be enough for them to be successful academically. For these students, Tier 2 interventions are necessary and can be effective at meeting their needs. Although interventions will vary by grade level and content area (i.e., reading, writing, and mathematics), there are five key elements of Tier 2 interventions:

1. Using data to identify students in need of Tier 2 interventions
2. Grouping students in small groups for intervention
3. Conducting intervention
4. Monitoring student progress
5. Reflecting on data and making decisions

To compare and contrast what Tier 2 is and what it is not, see Figure 4.1.

In this chapter, these components are described and examples are provided for various grade levels and content areas. However, because much of the research in RTI has focused on reading, you will note that each section is weighted more heavily with reading examples; when appropriate and the research literature supports it, examples from other content areas are provided. As you go through the chapter please refer to Figure 4.2 to guide your thoughts on how you will implement Tier 2 in your school or district.

FIGURE 4.2 *Guide to Effective RTI Implementation: Tier 2*

Who Is Responsible?	
Necessary Professional Development (For whom and by whom)	
Modification(s) and/or Intervention(s)	
Length of Time	
Teacher-Pupil Ratio	
Assessments Needed	
Assessments Used	
Frequency of Progress Monitoring	
Treatment Fidelity Observation	

(Continued)

FIGURE 4.2 *Continued*

Review of Modification(s) and/or Intervention(s)	
Parent Involvement	
Forms/Resources	

Using Data to Select Students in Need of Intervention

In Tier 1, students are assessed regularly; this is usually termed *universal screening* because all students are assessed to examine progress. This generally takes place at least 3–4 times a year, but sometimes more frequently. Using the data from universal screening tools, teachers can determine which students are making adequate growth in specific skills and which may be at-risk and in need of more intensive interventions in Tier 2. Although many schools and districts have measures that are given regularly, often these are measures that determine if students have mastered specific standards that have been taught. They do not necessarily measure the strengths or needs in skills that will impact more broad academic success such as reading fluency, reading comprehension, math computation, word problems, algebra, spelling, and written expression.

Curriculum-Based Measurements (CBM)

Curriculum-based measurements (CBM) are tools that are often used in RTI models because they have several useful features that allow them to be employed for both universal screening as well as progress monitoring. First, CBM are widely available and well-researched tools for collecting ongoing data during intervention (Wallace, Espin, McMasters, Deno, & Foegen, 2007). Second, the measurements were created to be reliable, valid, and practical so that teachers can administer the assessments quickly and interpret the scores of the assessments easily (Deno, 1985). Third, CBM provide educators with data to determine if an intervention is effective; that is, it shows whether students are making progress. They also provide individual student data so teachers can adjust instruction to meet the needs of their student (Deno, 1985). CBM measure students' initial performance and show progress on a particular skill. Small changes in student growth are revealed even if the student has not yet reached mastery of the skill (Fuchs, Fuchs, & Hamlett, 1993). This distinguishes CBM from other types of assessments that are often mastery

measures. Mastery assessments only give students credit if they have mastered the skill and therefore they do not show changes over short periods of time. CBM often have multiple forms of the same measure so that teachers can administer screening and progress monitoring assessments multiple times. They generally have established benchmarks that can be used to make decisions. In Figures 4.3, Figure 4.4, and Figure 4.5, there are lists of CBM for reading, math, and writing, including the grade levels for which these measures are appropriate.

Although CBM have been found to be reliable and valid measures, when using these measures with English learners, we need to be cautious in selecting and interpreting the results of these assessments. There is a small amount of research literature that supports using reading CBM, particularly oral reading fluency measures with second language learners (Wayman, Wallace, & Wiley, 2007). Additionally, DIBELS English measures such as letter naming fluency, phoneme segmentation fluency, and nonsense word fluency have been found to be useful in predicting later reading achievement for English learner populations (Graves, Plasencia-Peinado, Deno, & Johnson, 2005; Vanderwood, Kinklater, & Healy, 2008).

However, CBM tools have not been used extensively with English learners, and therefore established benchmarks and cutoffs may not be appropriate for this population of students. There are a couple of solutions to this problem. One is to assess students in both English and their native language. For example, there are reading fluency measures available in English and Spanish (see Figure 4.3 DIBELS/IDEL and AIMSweb measures). Assessing students in both languages can be useful because English learners may have certain skills in Spanish but may not be able to demonstrate these same skills in English because they have not had enough time to develop them. As an example, see Case Study 1 in Figure 4.6. On the other hand, by assessing students in both languages, teachers may find that the student struggles to read in both languages and is not developing English

FIGURE 4.3 *Curriculum-Based Measurement Reading*

Measure	Skills Assessed	Grade Levels
Dynamic Indicators of Basic Early Literacy Skills (DIBELS) Also available in Spanish–Indicadores Dinámicos del Éxito en la Lectura (IDEL) (https://dibels.uoregon.edu/)	Phonemic Awareness Alphabetic Principle Reading Fluency Comprehension (Retell) Vocabulary (Word Use)	K–6 (English) K–3 (Spanish)
Curriculum-Based Measurement in Reading (CBM-R) http://www.rti4success.org/chart/progressMonitoring/PMToolsChart_081109.pdf	Alphabetic Principle Reading Fluency Comprehension (MAZE)	K–7
AIMSweb-Reading www.aimsweb.com	Phonemic Awareness Alphabetic Principle Reading Fluency (Spanish & English) Comprehension (MAZE)	K–8 1–8 (Spanish Passage Fluency)

FIGURE 4.4 *CBM Math*

Measure	Skills Assessed	Grade Levels
AIMSweb www.aimsweb.com	Early Numeracy Math Computation Math Concepts and Applications	K–8
mClass-Math www.wirelessgeneration.com	Early Numeracy Math Computation Math Concepts	K–3
Project AAIMS Algebra Progress Monitoring Measures www.ci.hs.iastate.edu/aaims	Algebra	7 and up
Monitoring Basic Skills Progress (MBSP)	Math Computation Math Concepts	1–6

language skills as quickly as other English learners. These students are likely in need of intervention. As an example, see Case Study 2 in Figure 4.6.

If students speak a language other than Spanish or they have few reading skills in their primary language, this may not be an adequate solution. Alternatively, instead of using benchmarks provided by the measurement tool, it is possible to create local norms if assessments are done across a grade level in a whole school or district. Available programs

FIGURE 4.5 *CBM Writing*

Measure	Skills Assessed	Grade Levels
AIMSweb	Spelling Written Expression (scored as total words written, correct word sequences, words spelled correctly)	1–8
Early Writing Measures http://progressmonitoring.org/ probes/earlywriting.html	Sentence Copying Written Expression	1

FIGURE 4.6 *Case Studies Showing Two Typical Student Profiles*

Case 1: Julio	Case 2: Miguel
Julio came to Washington Elementary School mid-year in grade 2. He attended school in Mexico prior to moving to the U.S. His teacher assessed him in Spanish and English, in phonological awareness, the alphabetic principle, and reading fluency. Based on the benchmarks provided by the measurement tool, he was considered at grade level in Spanish, but at-risk in English. His teacher decided that she would observe him closely during Tier 1 instruction and make sure he was making progress. She regularly assessed him in both languages over the course of 10 weeks. During this time, he made a small amount of growth in Spanish, which is to be expected since the instruction he was receiving was in English. In English he made significant growth and was just below the grade-level benchmark. He also made large gains in his English language proficiency. His teacher and the grade 2 team decided that he would not need to be provided Tier 2 intervention.	Miguel came to Lincoln Elementary in the middle of grade 2 and had been attending school in Mexico. His teacher assessed him in English and Spanish, in phonological awareness, the alphabetic principle, and reading fluency. Based on the benchmarks provided by the measurement tool, he was considered at-risk in both English and Spanish. Additionally, his teacher noted he was not making much progress in English language proficiency. His teacher monitored his progress over 10 weeks in both English and Spanish. Over the course of the 10 weeks, data showed that he was not making adequate gains in English or Spanish reading, or in his English proficiency. His teacher and the grade 2 team decided he needed to be provided Tier 2 intervention.

such as AIMSweb allow local benchmarks to be established easily with their data management systems.

Besides employing assessments that measure academic progress, it is critical that we also examine second language acquisition in English learners, using an assessment of English language proficiency. Level of English proficiency should not be the deciding factor about whether a student needs Tier 2 intervention, because English learners can benefit from intervention even if they are not proficient in English (Gersten, et al., 2007; Richards & Leafstedt, 2010). However, English proficiency should be a consideration. For example, if a student has very low English language skills, team members may decide they want to give the student time to acquire those skills before making judgments about academic interventions. On the other hand, if the team members feel that this student is very quickly falling behind, they may decide that they want to immediately begin intervention. Bilingual staff and English Language Development specialists will be extremely critical members of this team as these decisions are made. As described in Chapter 1, a key feature in successful RTI models is teachers working together and examining data as a team (Haagar & Mahdavi, 2007). These teams work collaboratively to make decisions to determine which students are in need of Tier 2 intervention.

An Example of a Tier 2 Intervention Process at the Elementary School Level

Throughout the rest of this chapter we will follow a grade 5 teacher, Ms. Caliari, and her class at Rodriguez Elementary School, along with the grade 5 team as they implement Tier 2 in their school's RTI model. (Figure 4.7 describes how this process differs at the

FIGURE 4.7   *What about Tier 2 at the Secondary Level?*

There is research indicating that adolescents do benefit from intervention (Scammacca, et al., 2007). Many of the important features that are in the process for the 5th grade example apply to all grade levels, including secondary levels. For example, collecting data on student progress, using data to make instructional decisions, and providing small-group intervention are key principles of intervention at the secondary level (Kamil, et al., 2008). However, there are also some differences in how Tier 2 might look at the secondary level, particularly regarding collaboration across teachers and logistical decisions. For example, teachers at each grade level within language arts and math will need time to collaborate with each other and the intervention teachers to examine data and make decisions about who needs intervention and then to design the intervention. Furthermore, secondary schools need to examine how classes will be scheduled to ensure that students get the intervention they need, but also have the opportunity to exit intervention during various points in a semester.

In secondary schools, measures should be chosen that are related to the grade level of the students (see Figures 4.3–4.5). Data should be analyzed for each grade level and students at-risk need to be looked at individually to determine if they need intervention. Moreover, behavioral data may be useful to examine for secondary students in combination with academic data when making intervention decisions.

Many secondary students who need intervention are going to be several grade levels behind and will need intensive interventions in order for them to make necessary growth. Keeping groups small is one way to increase the intensity of the intervention, but secondary students also may need interventions that are 45 minutes each day and intervention sessions that are several weeks longer than what is needed at the elementary level, i.e., 12 weeks (Denton, et al., 2008). These interventions should be delivered by specialists or other trained teachers who understand reading development and struggling readers at the secondary level (Kamil et al., 2008). Interventions that only include limited skill development such as reading fluency are not likely to result in better outcomes for secondary students (Wexler, Vaughn, Roberts, & Denton, 2009). These students need intensive interventions that include both word level, text level, and strategy instruction (Kamil, et al., 2008). Although content area teachers are not likely to be delivering the interventions, they can support struggling readers in Tier 1 by providing advance organizers or other methods for making content text more accessible.

secondary level.) In Figure 4.8, you will find a partial class list of data from Ms. Caliari's class. Her grade 5 team meets twice a month, and during this meeting in late October, team members are making decisions about which students in this grade are in need of Tier 2 reading intervention. Each teacher uses a data sheet (seen in Figure 4.8) to keep track of class data and to examine individual student data. In September and October, the teachers administered both reading fluency and reading comprehension measures to students. In making decisions, the team considers these data as well as the previous year's state testing results and English proficiency.

The Rodriguez Elementary School grade 5 team includes: Ms. Caliari, Ms. Martinez, Ms. Nguyen, and Ms. Catwell. Mr. Correon, the bilingual specialist, and Ms. Shin, the Resource Specialist (special education teacher), also join the team meeting. Ms. Caliari's grade 5 team examines her class data closely. The Bilingual Specialist and the Resource Specialist also attend the meeting to provide additional consultation on which students need Tier 2 intervention. In examining the data, the team notices several students who are not meeting the benchmark on the critical reading skills of fluency and comprehension and who are not at the proficient level on the state test. These students fall into two groups: one group of students is not meeting grade-level benchmarks on fluency or comprehension (Vanessa, Leann, Francesca), and the second group is meeting benchmark in fluency, but not in comprehension (Maribel, Andy, Cindy, Russell, Tatyanna). The team also notices that there are two English learners in each of the two groups (Group 1: Vanessa, Francesca; Group 2: Maribel, Andy). For all students, but English learners in particular, it is critical to examine both the areas of strength and need so that the strengths

FIGURE 4.8 *Partial Data Sheet from Ms. Caliari's Grade 5 Class: Fall Trimester*

Student Name	English Language Proficiency Level	State Testing Designation	Oral Reading Fluency Goal = 104 words per minute (End of year 124)	MAZE Comprehension Goal = 20 (End of year 25)
Gabriel	Advanced	Proficient	110	30
Triet	Proficient	Proficient	120	35
Megan	EO	Proficient	112	28
Vanessa	Advanced	Below Basic	93	8
Maribel	Proficient	Basic	118	15
Juana	Fluent English Proficient (exited from EL status)	Proficient	118	27
Leann	EO	Far Below Basic	68	2
Alma	Fluent English Proficient (exited from EL status)	Proficient	112	33
Joseph	EO	Proficient	137	28
Andy	Advanced	Basic	114	17
Andrew	EO	Basic	110	27
Christopher	Fluent English Proficient (exited from EL status)	Proficient	125	32
Cindy	Fluent English Proficient (exited from EL status)	Below Basic	110	18
Marissa	EO	Proficient	127	32
Francesca	Advanced	Far Below Basic	56	10
Arianna	Advanced	Proficient	118	30
Russell	EO	Basic	113	16
Tatyanna	Fluent English Proficient (exited from EL status)	Basic	130	14

can be built upon and the areas of need can be targeted. The team decides to examine the assessments more closely to look at areas of strength and need for these students. Ms. Caliari and her team use the individual assessment data for each student to look at student strengths and needs, in order to determine how to group students for intervention. (See Figures 4.9 and 4.10.)

FIGURE 4.9 *Samples of Assessment Sheets from Francesca's Fall Trimester Assessments*

Oral Reading Fluency (1 minute; score is words per minute)

Student: Francesca   Date: September 10

They pushed the food ~~aside~~ *away*. "We can get something at the burger place after school," Ramon said.

They ~~concentrated~~ *skipped* on ~~studying~~ *stepping* for their English test ~~instead~~ *ins...* of eating. English was next period, and

Mr. ~~Friedman~~ *fttt...* had a ~~reputation~~ *skipped* for giving difficult tests. When the bell rang, they dropped their

~~uneaten~~ *skipped* lunches into the garbage. Mr. ~~Friedman~~ *skipped* was standing ~~nearby~~ *nare*. "Not hungry, guys?" he asked.

They | shook their heads and hurried off to class.

From Why the Sky is Far Away

(From Pearson Longman)

One student they discuss is Francesca. Francesca's fluency scores indicate that she can read sight words and some multisyllabic words. However, she struggles with complex words that contain prefixes and suffixes and does not appear to use a strategy for decoding the words, but instead guesses. The MAZE passage results indicate that she may understand that the paragraph is about soccer, a "sport." However, it appears that she lacks vocabulary that will help her understand the details of the passage. Additionally, her fluency assessments show that she is a slow reader and that she makes many reading errors, which can contribute to a lack of comprehension.

FIGURE 4.10 *MAZE Passage*

MAZE Passage (2.5 minutes; score is words per minute)

Student: Francesca   Date: 9-10-09

Brazil is the home of many left/(great)/notice soccer players, including the most famous

doctor/(factor)/player of all, Pelé. With his fast footwork/(consider)/decision, dazzling speed, and great

scoring ability, Pelé/(played)/forest/little for many years in Brazil and/(first)/then/night later in New York.

During his 22 notes/(paths)/years in soccer, he scored 1,281 goals hat/and/(from) held every major record

for the/(sport)/rough/strap.

From Popular Sports from Around the World by Kathy Mormile

(From Pearson Longman)

Note: These are only partial, rather than complete, passages.

Grouping Students in Small Groups for Intervention

When considering the three students in Ms. Caliari's class who are low on the fluency and comprehension measures (Vanessa, Leann, Francesca), the team decides that both Leann and Francesca are definitely in need of Tier 2 intervention that includes fluency and comprehension components. Vanessa did not meet benchmarks in either fluency or comprehension, but is not too far below the benchmark in fluency. Looking at Vanessa's individual assessment results, the team notices Vanessa makes very few errors in oral reading. Based on these data, the team decides that more intensive intervention focusing on comprehension will be most beneficial for her. However, Ms. Caliari will administer assessments regularly to ensure that Vanessa's fluency increases without specified fluency intervention.

The team also notes that four of the five students who met the benchmark in fluency but did not meet the benchmark in comprehension (Maribel, Cindy, Russell, and Tatyanna), will be provided Tier 2 intervention in comprehension, along with Vanessa. Andy has met the benchmark in oral reading fluency and is just shy of the benchmark for comprehension. He is also an advanced level English learner, and, in looking at his data provided by the Bilingual Specialist, the team notices that Andy has made growth in English proficiency since he came to Rodriguez School in grade 3 as a beginning level English speaker. After discussion, the team decides that they will not provide Andy with Tier 2 intervention at this time, but will examine his growth carefully over the next couple of months. Ms. Caliari will administer MAZE measures monthly for the next three months to determine if he is making necessary growth in comprehension and English proficiency.

After the team completes the data-driven decision-making process with Ms. Caliari's student data, they then continue discussing the other teachers' class data as they determine who needs Tier 2 intervention. The teachers move students around among each other for reading intervention and in order to make groups. Another teacher, Ms. Martinez, has two students, Carla and Tasha, who have similar needs to Francesca and Leann, so these students are provided intervention together. At Rodriguez, the special education teachers and bilingual specialists provide additional support to classroom teachers for intervention. In this case Ms. Shin, the RSP teacher, will be providing intervention to the group of grade 5 students who struggle with fluency and comprehension. Ms. Caliari provides intervention to the other five students in her class who need comprehension intervention (Vanessa, Maribel, Cindy, Russell, Tatyanna). Ms. Martinez, Ms. Nguyen, and Ms. Cartwell also have groups of 4–5 students who have comprehension needs. These teachers decide to each conduct the intervention with the students in their classrooms, but to plan intervention together so that all groups of students are receiving a similar intervention. At their meeting next week, they will begin planning, and get input from Ms. Shin and Mr. Correon during this planning time. The teachers spend the remaining time brainstorming when the best time of the day to conduct the interventions will be and what the other 25 students will be doing at that time. They decide that they will use the 30 minutes right after the language arts block to do intervention and that the other students will work on independent writing activities during this time. The team also decides that Ms. Caliari should have the support of a bilingual paraprofessional at the school site to help monitor the students who are working independently, since she has many students who have difficulty staying on-task (see Figure 4.11 for more information on how to use paraprofessionals to support

FIGURE 4.11 *The Role of Paraprofessionals in RTI*

There are limited paraprofessionals in the example provided for the 5th grade team at Rodriguez Elementary School. This team has one paraprofessional who is bilingual and the RSP teacher has a paraprofessional. The RSP teacher's paraprofessional spends time in the general education classrooms of other grade levels, supporting students with disabilities, while the RSP teacher works with her 5th grade small group. The bilingual paraprofessional manages the other students who are working independently while the Ms. Caliari is working with the students in Tier 2 intervention.

This is only one example of the role of paraprofessionals in an RTI model. At some schools with multiple paraprofessionals, these educators are important resources who can provide extra support in an RTI model. Often when schools have multiple paraprofessionals, there is a tendency to use these valuable assets to deliver intervention, particularly when the paraprofessionals speak the students' first language. However, it is important to emphasize two points. First, paraprofessionals should never be fully responsible for designing and delivering intervention for students, particularly for making instructional decisions about students in the absence of close collaboration with the certified teachers. Second, if paraprofessionals are going to assist in providing interventions, they need specific professional development in the content and methods of the intervention, progress monitoring, and collaboration (Hauerwas & Goessling, 2008). In order to ensure that English learners are provided the opportunity to make progress with Tier 2 intervention, the interventions need to be high quality and delivered with high fidelity. Ideally, we want the expert teachers who know both the content area, e.g., literacy, and English learner issues providing the interventions to the students who are in most need.

intervention). This is just one option for how to organize intervention. There are other processes that districts have implemented across the country.

The grade 5 team at Rodriguez Elementary grouped students for intervention based on data from screening measures and students' strengths and needs. Students should be grouped by skills and not by language level, as the heterogeneity of the language levels will be beneficial to the students. Additionally, the teachers put students in small groups, generally comprising 4–5 students. Small groups are sometimes defined as between 3–10 students. However, research on grouping configurations has shown that groups of 4–7 are very effective and that groups with more than 7 students do not make gains as great as smaller groups (Elbaum, Vaughn, & Hughes, 1999). Further, one-on-one instruction does not show additional benefits compared to small groups of 4–7. Groups of 4–5 are ideal for Tier 2 intervention because they are small enough to meet individual needs and also allow students to learn from each other. This is particularly important for English learners because it is critical that they have opportunities for interaction (Echevarria, Vogt, & Short, 2010a).

Conducting Small Group Intervention

In conducting intervention for English learners, both academic skill development and language development need to be considered. Conducting intervention involves both the content to be taught and the methods by which the content is delivered. Intervention provides students with the pre-skills they need to be successful, and teaches these skills to mastery. It does not involve "dumbing down" the curriculum for students, but instead simplifies tasks so that students are able to develop fully the skills critical for academic success. During intervention, teachers continue to use the techniques and methods described in Chapter 3 to make content accessible and develop language proficiency.

Content of Intervention

The content of intervention is going to vary greatly by grade level and according to students' needs and whether those involve reading, writing, or math. In determining content for intervention, teachers should teach essential skills that are necessary for overall academic success, as well as for ongoing development of these skills. Understanding the development of reading, writing, and mathematics skills and concepts is critical for teachers who are delivering intervention, as struggling students often need to be taught foundational skills in order to be able to perform at grade level. Additionally, content of the intervention should be based on data. Data from screening assessments can provide teachers with information on the individual strengths and areas of need. It is not within the scope of this chapter or book to describe all the possible content of interventions, but in Figure 4.12 you will find a sample lesson created for the students who are provided intervention by Ms. Shin (Francesca, Leann, Carla, & Tasha).

Figure 4.12   Sample Lesson

Lesson #5   Students Present: Francesca, Carla, Leann, Tasha

Tier 2-Group 2

Word Working	Vocabulary Development	Fluency Practice*	Comprehension*
Advanced decoding/spelling: Multisyllabic words, with suffixes -ed, -ing, -able, -less	Word roots: -port, -ject with prefixes (im, in, re, sub, de) *these prefixes (im, in, re, sub, de) were taught previously in word working activities	Repeated Reading (3-paragraph passage incorporating multi-syllabic words with suffixes, and words with targeted roots; one paragraph read at a time) 1. Modeled by teacher 2. Teacher and students read together 3. Student reads independently	Skill: Summarizing First paragraph summary modeled by teacher with think-aloud. Second paragraph read and summarized together. Third paragraph read and summarized independently.

*Suffixes and roots taught in word working, and vocabulary are in passages read for fluency and comprehension.

Methods of Delivering Instruction

Tier 2 intervention research indicates that intervention should be approximately 30 minutes per day. Obviously, this is going to depend greatly on the age and grade level of the students. For example, for kindergarteners you might break 30 minutes into two, 15-minute sessions. Intervention in Tier 2 is more effective when specific methods for delivering the

content are used (see Gersten, et al., 2007). These methods are critically important regardless of the content being taught. One specific method for delivering content is using a direct instruction approach called the Core Intervention Model (CIM) (Gerber, et al., 2004; Richards & Leafstedt, 2010). A significant advantage of using the CIM is that the teacher delivering the intervention can meet the needs of individual students in a small group. Therefore, students get individual needs met while also having the opportunity to learn from other students. There are six principles in the CIM, and they are aligned to the eight components of the SIOP® Model (see Figure 4.13).

FIGURE 4.13 *Alignment of CIM Principles with SIOP® Components*

Six CIM Principles	*Eight SIOP® Components and specific features*
Small groups	Interaction-grouping configurations
Set specific objectives	Lesson Preparation: Content and Language Objectives
Content and materials are appropriate	Lesson Preparation: Supplementary Materials, Adaptation of Content, Meaningful Activities
Explicit and intensive teaching of skills	Building Background—concepts linked to past learning Comprehensible Input—speech, clear explanation of tasks, using a variety of techniques Strategies—teaching learning strategies Practice & Application—hands-on materials and manipulatives, integrating language skills, Lesson Delivery—pacing
Explicit correction procedures	Strategies—Scaffolding strategies Review & Assessment—regular feedback
Opportunities for many correct responses	Interaction—opportunities for interaction with students and teacher Lesson Delivery—student engagement

Principle 1: Small Groups

The use of small groups has been described in detail previously.

Principle 2: Setting Objectives

Setting specific objectives requires that goals for students be established for the intervention, with specific daily objectives for each lesson. Objectives are based on student needs and the critical skills necessary for academic success in a particular content area. According to the SIOP® Model, both content and language objectives should be developed for intervention, as well as for regular classroom instruction. In order to have meaningful content and language objectives for intervention, they must be observable and measurable. This means that the teacher needs to observe the student "doing" the behavior and then be able to determine if the student has met the objective. See Figure 4.14 for sample content and language objectives for students in Ms. Shin's intervention group.

FIGURE 4.14 *Sample Content and Language Objectives*

Content Objectives	Language Objectives
Students will identify multisyllabic words with suffixes -*ed*, -*ing*, -*able*, -*less*.	Students will accurately read multisyllabic words with suffixes -*ed*, -*ing*, -*able*, -*less* in a passage.
Students will define words with the roots -*port* and -*ject*.	Students will write a 3 sentence summary of a passage after reading it aloud, using words with the suffixes -*port* and -*ject*.

Principle 3: Content and Materials Are Appropriate for a Student's Ability

In planning for intervention, the content and materials selected must be *appropriate* for each individual student's ability, meaning they should specifically target the student's individual needs. At times, this means that individual students in a group may require different content and materials even though they are working toward the same objective and are participating in the same activities. For example, in the summarizing activity, all students are working toward the same objective: summarizing the passage in three sentences. Leann, Carla, and Tasha may all be writing summaries using a list of key words such as "First, Next, Finally." However, Francesca may need more support and may be given sentence frames such as "First the family . . . , Next, the girl . . . , Finally, her brother . . ."

Principle 4: Skills Must Be Taught Explicitly, Intensively, and at a Rapid Pace

Explicit teaching involves modeling, breaking tasks and skills into steps, guided practice, and independent practice. Intensive intervention involves group size, additional time, and pacing. To provide students intensive intervention, group size must be small and students need to have adequate time in addition to general classroom instruction that is dedicated to intervention. To increase the intensity of intervention, the teacher can make the group smaller or add additional time (Vaughn, Wanzek, Woodruff, & Linan-Thompson, 2007). Intensive intervention also needs to be conducted at a rapid pace, so the lessons need to move quickly. Rapid pacing is critical because students who are struggling have fallen behind their peers, which means that they need to learn much more in a shorter amount of time (Engelman, Becker, Carnine, & Gersten, 1988). Rapid pace requires students to respond frequently; therefore, there is less time for distraction or inattention, which tends to occur more often with students who need intervention.

Principle 5: Students Must Be Provided Opportunities for Many Correct Responses

During intervention, teachers need to maximize the number of correct response opportunities for each student. Students in need of intervention often do not do not take the risk to respond, or, when they do respond, they are often deemed incorrect. Therefore, during

intervention, these students need to have many opportunities to respond. To maximize the number of student responses, Ms. Caliari provides opportunities for students to respond in a variety of ways. She uses choral responses, and provides opportunities for students to respond individually or interact with each other in responses. For example, Ms. Caliari might have the students read summaries to a partner. Ms. Caliari also reinforces students when they respond correctly. She might say, "Francesca, that is correct. *Unrest* means *not at rest*, because *un* means *not*." As in the example, it is important that intervention teachers use deliberate and systematic praise.

Principle 6: Corrective Feedback Using the Staircase Approach

In the Core Intervention Model, explicit correction procedures are the crux of the model. Students are praised for correct responses. When an incorrect answer is given, students are led to the correct answer while the incorrect response is ignored. After an incorrect response, students are provided the opportunity to respond immediately to a simplified question or task. Correction procedures involve using the staircase approach to correct students during instruction. The staircase approach ensures that students are led to the correct answer and are given the opportunity to respond independently to the original task. As a teacher takes the student down the steps in the staircase, he or she must take the student back up. Figure 4.15 shows an example of a staircase for decoding vowel combinations. For much more detail on using the staircase approach and the other principles of the CIM, see Richards & Leafstedt (2010).

Monitoring Student Progress

Students in Tier 2 receive five days of intervention each week for approximately 30 minutes during each day. Each intervention session should last about 8–10 weeks. During intervention, progress monitoring data are collected to make modifications to intervention

FIGURE 4.15 *Example of Staircase Approach for Providing Corrective Feedback Lesson Content Objective*

Content Objective:
Students will identify (or point to) words that have two vowels together in the middle of words (vowel combinations).

Language Objective:
Students will read words with two vowels together in words (vowel combinations) to see if the first vowel says its name.

Step 1: Original question or task: "Read this sentence: *The boat made it back to the dock."*

Step 2: Prompt for a re-read: "Put your finger on the word that begins with *b*. Read the word again."

Step 3: Prompt for a specific part/decoding correctly/decoding incorrectly/rule: "What sound do the letters */oa/* make in the word *boat*? Remember that in many words, when two vowels are next to each other, the first one says its name."

Step 4: Ask yes/no question: "Does */oa/* make the "ō" sound?"

Step 5: Tell the answer: "*/oa/* makes the sound "ō." What sound?"

Step 6: Say and have student repeat: "The word is *boat*. Say it. Read it."

and to determine if the intervention is, in fact, working for the students. It is absolutely critical that student progress be monitored regularly during intervention in an RTI model. This is even more critical for English learners who are rapidly developing both academic and language skills because teachers can readily adapt instruction with current data. Additionally, progress monitoring data provide teachers with information about who may need to continue or exit intervention.

Currently the best method we have for collecting progress monitoring data during intervention is by using Curriculum Based Measurements. For students in Tier 2 interventions, progress monitoring should take place at least 1–2 times each month. Weekly progress monitoring is ideal because it allows teachers to use these data to make changes to instruction. However, many teachers find it difficult to find additional time for progress monitoring. Therefore, it is recommended that teachers use one day of intervention every two weeks to assess students. For example, Ms. Caliari provides 30 minutes of intervention each day for the first week, but during the second week she provides intervention for four days, and reserves that 30-minute block on Friday to assess each student in the group.

For students in Tier 2, generally grade-level CBM are appropriate, but at times students will be performing below grade level, and intervention will be provided in content that addresses skills students need to reach grade level. In this case, a student may not show any growth on a grade-level assessment even though he or she is making progress. Therefore, monitoring progress at the student's level of performance is appropriate. For example, if Francesca is receiving instruction that is giving her the skills she needs for grade 5, but she is technically reading at the grade 4 level, then regular progress monitoring using grade 4 CBM is appropriate. However, periodically, grade-level measures should also be given to see if grade-level improvement is being made. Francesca's progress monitoring graphs over ten weeks are shown in Figures 4.16 and 4.17. Note that she is making some progress in on grade 4 fluency passages, but has essentially not made any progress in grade 4 comprehension. Additionally, she has made only slight progress on grade 5 fluency, and no progress on grade 5 comprehension.

Compare Francesca's data to Tatyanna's. Tatyanna, who is only receiving intervention in comprehension, has made tremendous growth after ten weeks of intervention in grade 5

FIGURE 4.16 *Francesca's Fluency Progress over 10 Weeks of Intervention*

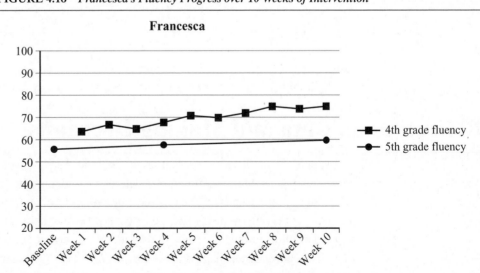

FIGURE 4.17 *Francesca's Comprehension Progress over the 10 Weeks of Intervention*

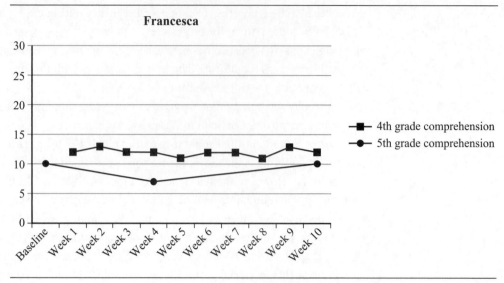

FIGURE 4.18 *Tatyanna's Fluency Progress over the 10 Weeks of Intervention*

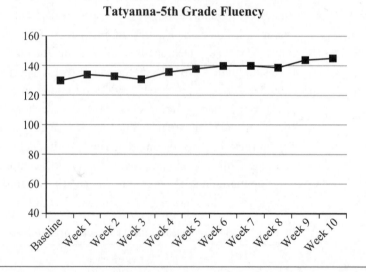

comprehension, and her fluency continues to increase on pace with grade-level bench-marks, despite not receiving specific intervention in fluency (see Figures 4.18 and 4.19).

Reflecting on Data and Making Decisions

At the end of the 10-week intervention session, the grade 5 team at Rodriguez Elementary examines the progress monitoring data of all students who were in intervention and also looks at the second trimester of screening data. A second trimester of screening data is conducted to determine if there are students who may have fallen behind and are now in need of intervention, even though they did not receive it during the first trimester.

The team first considers progress monitoring data for students who previously received Tier 2 interventions. Schools should consider having some rules about how

FIGURE 4.19 *Tatyanna's Comprehension Progress over the 10 Weeks of Intervention*

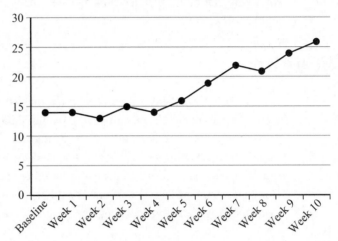

Tatyanna 5th Grade Comprehension

changes to students' intervention can be made. For students who have received one session of Tier 2 intervention, there are three options: (1) Students have made adequate progress and reached benchmarks, and they can return to general Tier 1 instruction (which again is sheltered, differentiated, and meets the needs of the majority of students); (2) Students may have made some progress, but need an additional round of Tier 2 intervention, so they will receive an additional 8–10 week session; and (3) Students have made very little progress in the Tier 2 intervention and need to be considered for more intensive intervention in Tier 3.

First, the grade 5 team at Rodriguez Elementary examines Ms. Caliari's class and they determine that Tatyanna, Andy, Maribel, and Russell no longer are in need of Tier 2 interventions because they have shown growth and met benchmarks, but Ms. Caliari will monitor their progress monthly to make sure that they do not fall behind. They also decide that Leann, Cindy, and Vanessa will receive an additional session of Tier 2 intervention for another 10 weeks, which will focus mainly on comprehension. The team discusses Francesca's data for quite awhile, and they request consultation again from Ms. Shin, who worked with Francesca in intervention, and also from Mr. Correon, the bilingual specialist who provides ELD instruction to Francesca. Mr. Correon states that he is very worried about Francesca's lack of progress in ELD and has looked at her history, which indicates that she has been considered "Advanced" now for two years, but cannot exit English learner status. Ms. Shin states that she has made individual modifications to Francesca's intervention and believes she might benefit from a more intense intervention. The team decides that Francesca will receive a more intense intervention in Tier 3, and will be in a smaller group of 3 students during this intervention. She will also receive 45 minutes of intervention each day.

The second trimester screening data are discussed next to determine if any students who were not originally in need of Tier 2 intervention may now need intervention. The team then discusses how to regroup students, considering the additional students that now need intervention, and then begin again to look at individual data to create these groups and determine the content to be taught in the interventions. The grade 5 team at Rodriguez

Elementary illustrates how decisions can be made with grade-level or RTI teams; note how these decisions were made on an individual student basis. This is particularly important when considering English learners, because many factors may impact progress during intervention.

Final Thoughts

The five key components of Tier 2 interventions will ensure that students are selected appropriately for intervention, delivered the intervention they need with specific methods of delivery, and monitored carefully in their progress. Teachers who work in teams and include colleagues with specific backgrounds in second language acquisition and special education can make informed decisions based on data about English learners in need of Tier 2 intervention. These decisions should be made on an individual level and consider academic progress as well as language acquisition and proficiency.

For Reflection and Discussion

1. How can specialists, such as a bilingual teacher and a special education teacher, be helpful in making decisions about students?
2. What teaching methods are critical for delivering interventions for struggling English learners? Why?
3. How is regular progress monitoring useful for guiding intervention for individual students?

Tier 3 Interventions for English Learners

A culturally responsive RTI model has tremendous potential to . . . more appropriately differentiate between culturally and linguistically diverse learners who do and do not have true disabilities. Only by doing so can all children achieve their full potential.

Klinger, Sorrells, & Barrera, 2007, p. 239

Many English learners struggle academically, and as a group lag far behind their native English-speaking peers. Disproportionate numbers of English learners are referred to special education, with many either over- or underidentified as having learning disabilities (Artiles & Trent, 2007). It is quite a challenge to disentangle possible learning deficits from limited language proficiency, both in English and in their home language. In this complex situation, several profiles emerge that include, but are not limited to, the following (Echevarria & Graves, 2010):

English learners who are literate and fluent in their home language. These students have the tremendous advantage of having a foundation in literacy skills in their home language; with careful instruction, those skills will transfer to English. However, these English learners are still learning new concepts, information, and skills in a new language. There may be some areas where they struggle because of the cognitive demand required to process information in a new language. In some cases, as students have reported in our research, they simply do not understand the teacher. As we discuss in Chapter 3, it is critical that teachers use teaching techniques and practices that make both the content and the language (English) comprehensible for their students.

English learners who speak their native language fluently but are not literate in it. These students do not have a reservoir of academic skills and concepts on which to draw as they are exposed to literacy development. Imagine how difficult it would be to learn a new, difficult concept such as nuclear fusion: the process by which multiple like-charged atomic nuclei join together to form a heavier nucleus. It is accompanied by the release or absorption of energy, which allows matter to enter a plasma state. You have the advantage of using background knowledge and experience to try to make sense of that definition, yet it may still be difficult for you to understand. Now picture having someone explain it to you in a language that you don't understand, or you understand a little, or you understand in conversation, but you are totally lost at this level of academic discussion. If the person speaks to you as if you are a native speaker of the language (doesn't repeat, show visuals to accompany words, or check for understanding, etc.), you would have great difficulty ever understanding nuclear fusion. Since you *do* have many successful learning experiences in your background, you would understand that it is a language issue, not one of intelligence, motivation, or some disability that prevents you from comprehending. However, English learners who have not had successful learning experiences and who thus do not have a reservoir of academic skills and concepts that help them make sense of new information will struggle even more. They would benefit from instruction in their first language to develop these critical literacy skills. If bilingual personnel are not available and instruction is in English, we must be extremely careful when attributing poor performance to factors such as low intelligence, lack of motivation, and learning disabilities. These students have not had sufficient opportunity to learn grade-level skills or to have material presented in a comprehensible way.

English learners—most of whom were born in the U.S.—who are "limited bilinguals" because they are not completely fluent in their home language and have not yet attained proficiency in English. More than 75% of elementary and 50%

of secondary English learners were born in the U.S. (Capps, et al., 2005), so they have been exposed to a mix of their home language and English for years before they enter school. Because many of these children are poor (Garcia & Jensen, 2007), they most likely do not come from homes where literacy activities are part of the daily fabric of their lives. According to the 2000 U.S. census, of the parents of English learner children in elementary school, almost half had not completed high school, and a quarter had less than a ninth grade education (Ballantyne, Sanderman, & Levy, 2008). As a result, many English learners do not have a model of academic language in the home. The level of English they are exposed to, for example, on television and in conversation, is not the kind of language that is useful for completing rigorous, standards-based lessons and literacy development. When students "speak English," they are often expected to perform at grade level in English. However, they usually have significant gaps in their repertoire of skills since they didn't receive literacy instruction in their home language and they struggle to understand the English that is used in the classroom (Cummins, 2000). Again, instruction that is decontextualized (few or no clues), is not tied to their own experiences, and is presented in ways that are difficult to understand will not achieve the results the teacher intends. Many times, instruction lacks meaning for them, which can contribute to off-task behavior, low motivation, and apathy toward books and stories. These are also some of the characteristics of learning disabilities, which complicate the situation when students are not reaching benchmarks.

As you can see, each of the profiles discussed presents unique issues and instructional decisions. RTI offers an opportunity to give each student the kind of attention he or she needs to be successful through providing high-quality teaching, monitoring progress, making adaptations to enhance learning, documenting the adaptations and the results, providing intervention if needed, and continually monitoring the student's response to what has been tried.

In this chapter we discuss Tier 3 (or Tier 3 and beyond) and address its characteristics in the RTI process. We also present information on how to identify a learning disability (LD) and how to distinguish between LD and cultural and linguistic differences. Finally, we offer suggestions for conducting effective IEP meetings with English learners and their families. Tier 3 provides the most intensive and costly intervention schools offer. When looking for *the* answer to the many questions associated with RTI, it is important to keep in mind that there is limited evidence about the application of an RTI approach for English learners. However, it appears that using RTI with English learners will produce results that are similar to those achieved when using it with native English speakers (Vanderwood & Nam, 2007).

As you consider the issues discussed in this chapter and the context of your own district or school setting, please complete the Guide to Effective RTI Implementation for Tier 3 in Figure 5.6 found at the end of the chapter.

What Is Different about Tier 3?

While Tier 2 intervention provides a "boost" in that it supplements the teaching methods and materials used in general education and targets specific skill areas, Tier 3 uses a different

approach for meeting students' individual needs. One might consider Tier 3 akin to conducting an experiment on each student to determine what "effective instruction" is for that individual learner. Researcher Lynn Fuchs (2009) characterizes it in this way: "You have progress monitoring data, and you test the effectiveness of instructional components for a child. And you incorporate the ones that look effective for that child, and you drop other components that don't look effective. So it's experimental for that child."

For English learners, this experimental process would, when possible, include using the home language for literacy development. If that isn't possible, given the hundreds of languages represented in schools, at least clarifying instruction in the home language would be beneficial. Home language support might be provided by a bilingual instructional aide, a community volunteer, or as in some districts, by high school students who speak the language and receive community service hours for serving as instructional tutors/interpreters. Although it may be assumed that some level of home language support would have been part of Tier 1 instruction and Tier 2 intervention for English learner students, those services may not have been possible due to lack of bilingual personnel. However, best practice dictates that it is advisable that improved performance using the first language be explored before any label (i.e., learning disability) is ascribed to an English learner.

In some districts, Tier 3 is the most intense level of intervention provided to students in general education (a fourth tier would be special education services). In other districts, Tier 3 groups may include students who need intensive intervention along with students identified as having learning disabilities.

At Tier 3, the goal is remediation of existing problems and prevention of more severe problems (or secondary behavioral issues such as withdrawal, depression, or acting out) that often arise as a result of frustration and persistent underachievement. Tier 3 intervention is provided to students who do not make adequate progress after a reasonable amount of time with the Tier 2 interventions that were provided for them. These students require more intensive assistance. Tier 3 (or, in districts with more than three tiers, tiers 3 and above) entails individualized, intensive intervention. This increased intensity is characterized by using more systematic, explicit instruction that targets the students' skill deficits. It is done more frequently, and for longer duration. Instruction is provided in smaller groups, including one-on-one tutoring and more homogeneous groups by a teacher or specialist with greater expertise.

For example, the student discussed in Chapter 4, Francesca, did not make sufficient progress in comprehension or academic English after Tier 2 intervention, which she received every day (frequency) for 30 minutes in a group of 4–5 students (intensity) over the course of 10 weeks (duration). The team referred her to Tier 3 for more intensive intervention. In Tier 3, Francesca would be in a group with a maximum of 3 students for 45 minutes each day. During that time, the specialist would focus on providing intervention that specifically targeted building academic English while developing each student's comprehension skills. Progress would be monitored weekly to ascertain which components of the intervention are working and what changes need to be made to the materials and methods being used with Francesca. After 12 weeks, the team will meet and discuss Francesca's progress.

Since RTI is a recursive process (see Figure 1.2 in Chapter 1), it is possible that after Tier 3 intervention, Francesca would return to the general education program for 100% of her day. If needed, she would receive Tier 2 intervention to reinforce the progress made in Tier 3.

In this way, Tier 3 intervention offers the child a chance to remediate the problem before it becomes even more severe, and it may prevent behaviors common to underperforming English learners such as disengagement or poor attendance. For English learners, the person delivering the instruction would, at a minimum, have an understanding of second language acquisition and be familiar with the students' culture. Preferably she would be able to provide clarification and/or instructional support in the students' primary languages.

In a study of RTI, students who did not make progress at Tier 2 who would be eligible for Tier 3 services ranged from 2%–6% of the general school population (Torgesen, 2000). Schools with higher numbers of students who are in need of Tier 3 intervention should carefully examine the quality of their Tier 1 and Tier 2 services, particularly the general education classroom. Intervention supplements high-quality classroom instruction, and with English learners, the features of the SIOP® Model must be used with fidelity to improve achievement.

Some of the characteristics of Tier 3, as well as misconceptions, are reflected Figure 5.1.

Typically, intervention takes up a small part of the day and focuses on building specific skills that will enhance learning when they are in Tier 1 the rest of the day. For the majority of the school day English learners should be engaged in rich, meaningful discussion and activities around text; teaching techniques are used that encourage active participation and provide students with the support they need to be successful in each lesson. Even if English learners receive Tier 2 and Tier 3 intervention, instruction in the general education classroom must reflect best practice for them.

FIGURE 5.1 *Defining Tier 3*

Tier 3 is …	*Tier 3 is not …*
Strategic instruction that promotes learning for each student (including English language development), based on individual need. It is more intensive than Tier 2; is more teacher-centered, systematic, and explicit, with lots of opportunity for student participation; uses smaller, homogeneous groups; is provided more frequently; is conducted by instructors with greater expertise; and is implemented for longer duration.	Simply more of the same instruction students received in the core curriculum.
Intended for a specific duration of time using frequent progress monitoring to inform on-going decisions about placement.	A life sentence.
Part of a recursive RTI process where students move in and out of tiers, depending on their documented need for support. Students are in Tier 1 for most of the school day, even when they receive intervention.	A way to remove challenging students from general education.
A way to identify learning disabilities. Documentation that shows a student who is not making progress despite having been provided evidence-based instruction for English learners, targeted at specific skill development, delivered with fidelity in small groups by a teacher with expertise in literacy and English language development may indicate a learning disability.	Necessarily special education. Some RTI processes provide students with IEPs another tier of support, usually called Tier 4.

There are a number of evidence-based practices for teaching reading to English learners. Specific principles to guide reading instruction for Spanish-speaking students (Vaughn, et al., 2006) include:

- Designing programs based on commonalities between reading instruction in English and in Spanish;
- Making connections between students' knowledge in Spanish and its application to English;
- Organizing peer and cooperative groups to enhance learning;
- Providing multiple opportunities for students to use oral language in Spanish or English to respond to higher-order questions;
- Recognizing that English literacy will require more explicit instruction in both phonics and word reading.

There are also evidence-based practices specifically for teaching at-risk learners or students with learning disabilities in reading, math, writing, and behavior discussed in a special issue of *Exceptional Children* (2009). Specific interventions that have proven effective with English learners are discussed in Chapter 4 of this book. Finally, Cloud (2006) suggests practices for English learners who are receiving special education services that include use of cooperative learning, visual learning approaches, multisensory teaching approaches, experience-based learning (e.g., language experience approach; discovery learning), process-based teaching approaches (e.g., readers/writers workshop), and technology-based learning (e.g., interactive software, assistive technologies). These practices are represented in the features of the SIOP® Model.

We direct readers to these resources as you generate professional development plans for effective RTI in your school or district. But remember that instruction and intervention aren't the entire picture: Ongoing analysis of student performance data is critical, especially in Tier 3. Systematically collected data are used to identify successes and failures in instruction for individual students and adjustments are made frequently.

Identifying a Disability

One of the reasons RTI became an option for schools under the Individuals With Disabilities Education Improvement Act of 2004 (IDEA 2004) is that it is difficult to pinpoint with precision high-incidence disabilities such as learning disabilities (LD) or speech and language disorders. The situation is complicated with English learners since it is often difficult to determine if the student is struggling academically because of low English proficiency, because of some sort of language or learning disability, or because of another source.

At this point, there is no consensus in the field about what are the best RTI methods for disability identification. Some of the questions researchers have yet to answer include: Is there a need for formal testing or should we rely on student response to intervention as a basis for identification? Should RTI be used in combination with some formal measures? If so, which ones (Fuchs & Deshler, 2007)? These are only a few of the many questions left to be answered.

In current practice, students who do not achieve the desired level of progress in response to targeted interventions may be considered for eligibility for special education

services under the IDEA 2004 (see Appendix A). Level of progress would be determined by the student's rate of response to intervention and the size of the gap that exists between the student and the benchmark. Special education services would also be considered when it has been demonstrated that the intensity or type of intervention required to improve student performance either exceeds the resources in general education or is not available in general education settings.

The data collected during Tiers 1, 2, and 3 are included and used to make eligibility decisions. The advantage of using "hard" quantitative data for decision-making is that it may be more reliable than "soft" data sources such as teacher referral (Gersten & Dimino, 2006). For some English learners, their problems may include: they couldn't keep up with the rest of the class, especially in schools with large class numbers; they may have been taught improperly in the early grades; or they did not receive sufficient English language development. With RTI, those students can receive the academic attention they need in a small group setting and avoid an unnecessary referral to special education.

It is important to note, however, that at any point in an RTI process, IDEA 2004 allows parents to request a formal evaluation to determine eligibility for special education. An RTI process cannot be used to deny or delay a formal evaluation for special education. Nor should special education services be withheld because of a lack of English proficiency when a disability is indicated.

A Learning Disability Is Hard to Define

Although learning disabilities are common, affecting an estimated 4%–6% of the public school population (Horowitz, 2009), in most situations it can be difficult to identify a specific learning disability; it is not the same as having Downs syndrome or being visually impaired since those disabilities have a clear-cut diagnosis and biological characteristics. To date, the same is not true for learning disabilities. In fact, there is some argument that high-incidence disabilities such as learning disabilities (as well as behavior disorders and mild mental retardation) are socially constructed. That is, individual judgment is used to decide what is "normal" along a spectrum of behaviors and to determine at what point an individual is deemed "disabled" (Harry, Klinger, & Cramer, 2007; Ruiz, 1995).

The term *learning disabilities* is used to describe "mixed bag" of disorders that affect listening, speaking, reading, writing, reasoning, math, and social skills (Horowitz & Stecker, 2007). In an interview, Doug Fuchs (2009) reminds us that there isn't one specific characteristic—or even two or three—that typify a student who requires special education services, but it is usually a constellation of behaviors or symptoms, and the constellation changes as the child matures. For example, Fuchs mentions that young children have weak language functioning and very poor attention. He says, "They're distractible, they're disorganized, they are often off-task." As these children get older, they develop problematic behaviors such as low motivation, poor self-perception and negative attitudes toward learning.

Identifying a learning disability is more complicated when a student is culturally and linguistically diverse. In Figure 5.2, we show a comprehensive checklist of behaviors that provides guidance for determining a learning disability, developed through the National Center for Learning Disabilities (NCLD) (Horowitz & Stecker, 2007). We will discuss each domain in the context of language and cultural diversity. As you look over the checklist, you will see that there are many behaviors that apply to most people—even you! However, although most people experience problems with learning and behavior from time to time, a person with learning disabilities experiences these difficulties over their life

FIGURE 5.2 *Learning Disabilities Checklist of Signs and Symptoms*

Learning Disabilities Checklist

Domains and Behaviors *Shaded area indicates a characteristic is more likely to apply at that stage of life. Check all that apply.*	Preschool Kindergarten	Grades 1-4	Grades 5-8	High School & Adult
Gross and Fine Motor Skills				
Appears awkward and clumsy, dropping, spilling, or knocking things over				
Has limited success with games and activities that demand eye-hand coordination (e.g., piano lessons, basketball, baseball)				
Has trouble with buttons, hooks, snaps, zippers and trouble learning to tie shoes				
Creates art work that is immature for age				
Demonstrates poor ability to color or write 'within the lines'				
Grasps pencil awkwardly, resulting in poor handwriting				
Experiences difficulty using small objects or items that demand precision (e.g., Legos, puzzle pieces, tweezers, scissors)				
Dislikes and avoids writing and drawing tasks				
Language				
Demonstrates early delays in learning to speak				
Has difficulty modulating voice (e.g., too soft, too loud)				
Has trouble naming people or objects				
Has difficulty staying on topic				
Inserts invented words into conversation				
Has difficulty re-telling what has just been said				
Uses vague, imprecise language and has a limited vocabulary				
Demonstrates slow and halting speech, using lots of fillers (e.g., uh, um, and, you know, so)				
Uses poor grammar or misuses words in conversation				
Mispronounces words frequently				
Confuses words with others that sound similar				
Inserts malapropisms ('slips of the tongue') into conversation (e.g., a rolling stone gathers no moths; he was a man of great statue)				
Has difficulty rhyming				
Has limited interest in books or stories				
Has difficulty understanding instructions or directions				
Has trouble understanding idioms, proverbs, colloquialisms, humor, and/or puns (note: take into account regional and cultural factors)				

Domains and Behaviors *Shaded area indicates a characteristic is more likely to apply at that stage of life. Check all that apply.*	Preschool Kindergarten	Grades 1-4	Grades 5-8	High School & Adult
Language (con't)				
Has difficulty with pragmatic skills (e.g., understands the relationship between speaker and listener, stays on topic, gauges the listeners degree of knowledge, makes inferences based on a speaker's verbal and non-verbal cues)				
Reading				
Confuses similar-looking letters and numbers				
Has difficulty recognizing and remembering sight words				
Frequently loses place while reading				
Confuses similar-looking words (e.g., beard/bread)				
Reverses letter order in words (e.g., saw/was)				
Demonstrates poor memory for printed words				
Has weak comprehension of ideas and themes				
Has significant trouble learning to read				
Has trouble naming letters				
Has problems associating letter and sounds, understanding the difference between sounds in words or blending sounds into words				
Guesses at unfamiliar words rather than using word analysis skills				
Reads slowly				
Substitutes or leaves out words while reading				
Has poor retention of new vocabulary				
Dislikes and avoids reading or reads reluctantly				
Written Language				
Dislikes and avoids writing and copying				
Demonstrates delays in learning to copy and write				
Writing is messy and incomplete, with many cross outs and erasures				
Has difficulty remembering shapes of letters and numerals				
Frequently reverses letters, numbers and symbols				
Uses uneven spacing between letters and words, and has trouble staying 'on the line'				
Copies inaccurately (e.g., confuses similar-looking letters and numbers)				
Spells poorly and inconsistently (e.g., the same word appears differently other places in the same document)				

FIGURE 5.2 *Continued*

Learning Disabilities Checklist

Domains and Behaviors *Shaded area indicates a characteristic is more likely to apply at that stage of life. Check all that apply.*	Preschool Kindergarten	Grades 1-4	Grades 5-8	High School & Adult
Written Language (con't)				
Has difficulty proofreading and self-correcting work				
Has difficulty preparing outlines and organizing written assignments				
Fails to develop ideas in writing so written work is incomplete and too brief				
Expresses written ideas in a disorganized way				
Math				
Has difficulty with simple counting and one-to-one correspondence between number symbols and items/objects				
Difficulty mastering number knowledge (e.g. recognition of quantities without counting)				
Has difficulty with learning and memorizing basic addition and subtraction facts				
Has difficulty learning strategic counting principles (e.g. by 2, 5, 10, 100)				
Poorly aligns numbers resulting in computation errors				
Has difficulty estimating (e.g., quantity, value)				
Has difficulty with comparisons (e.g., less than, greater than)				
Has trouble telling time				
Has trouble conceptualizing the passage of time				
Has difficulty counting rapidly or making calculations				
Has trouble learning multiplication tables, formulas and rules				
Has trouble interpreting graphs and charts				
Social/Emotional				
Does not pick up on other people's mood/feelings (e.g., may say the wrong thing at the wrong time)				
May not detect or respond appropriately to teasing				
Has difficulty 'joining in' and maintaining positive social status in a peer group				
Has trouble knowing how to share/express feelings				
Has trouble 'getting to the point' (e.g., gets bogged down in details in conversation)				
Has difficulty with self-control when frustrated				
Has difficulty dealing with group pressure, embarrassment and unexpected challenges				
Has trouble setting realistic social goals				

Domains and Behaviors *Shaded area indicates a characteristic is more likely to apply at that stage of life. Check all that apply.*	Preschool Kindergarten	Grades 1-4	Grades 5-8	High School & Adult
Social/Emotional (con't)				
Has trouble evaluating personal social strengths and challenges				
Is doubtful of own abilities and is prone to attribute successes to luck or outside influences rather than hard work				
Attention				
Fails to pay close attention to details or makes careless mistakes in schoolwork, work, or other activities				
Has difficulty sustaining attention in work tasks or play activities				
Does not follow through on instructions and fails to finish schoolwork, chores, or duties in the workplace				
Has difficulty organizing tasks and activities				
Avoids, dislikes, or is reluctant to engage in tasks that require sustained mental effort such as homework and organizing work tasks				
Loses things consistently that are necessary for tasks/activities (e.g., toys, school assignments, pencils, books, or tools)				
Is easily distracted by outside influences				
Is forgetful in daily/routine activities				
Other				
Confuses left and right				
Has a poor sense of direction; slow to learn the way around a new place; easily lost or confused in unfamiliar surroundings				
Finds it hard to judge speed and distance (e.g., hard to play certain games, drive a car)				
Trouble reading charts and maps				
Is disorganized and poor at planning				
Often loses things				
Is slow to learn new games and master puzzles				
Has difficulty listening and taking notes at the same time				
Performs inconsistently on tasks from one day to the next				
Has difficulty generalizing (applying) skills from one situation to another				

span. When applying the checklist to an individual, the more characteristics you check, the more likely it is that the individual is at risk (or shows signs of) learning disabilities.

Gross and fine motor skills development would not be affected by language or cultural differences. However, lack of exposure to activities that demand hand-eye coordination or precision may have an impact on performance. With practice, for example, using scissors or playing sports, performance would be expected to improve.

In the area of language skills, characteristics of second language acquisition often mirror language/learning difficulties. Thus, it is critical to assess students suspected of learning disabilities in both the home language and English to ascertain performance levels (Echevarria & Graves, 2010; Ortiz, 1997; Salend & Salinas, 2003). Imagine that you have just recently relocated to another country. Take a look at the language characteristics listed in Figure 5.1 and think about how many of those would apply. Many English learners lack the auditory acuity to hear new, "foreign" sounds much like English speakers may have difficulty understanding the name of a person or place that contains sounds with which they are unfamiliar. Also, the cognitive and linguistic demands of learning through a language in which you are not fluent are tremendous. You would likely have difficulty staying on topic, using precise language, or understanding instructions when you are on cognitive overload. But the situation would be language-specific and would get better with time. Students with learning disabilities will manifest many of these characteristics in both languages—their home language and English—consistently and over time.

Reading is also an area that is certainly impacted by language proficiency. For example, it is difficult to remember letter names, words, or passages that have little or no meaning for you. We know from schema research that individuals with knowledge of a topic have better recall and are better able to elaborate on the topic than those with limited knowledge of the topic (Chiesi, Spilich, & Voss, 1979). For some English learners, their difficulty with reading may be more a function of lack of familiarity than inability to learn.

In young learners, some of the characteristics listed in the Written Language domain of Figure 5.1 may be the result of language differences. For example, difficulty remembering the shape of letters or reversing letters could be attributed to lack of exposure, especially when students are not familiar with the Roman alphabet. Older English learners may have difficulty organizing and expressing their thoughts in a coherent way in writing when they have less than fluent English proficiency.

Math is often referred to as the "universal language," but in reality there are a lot of math-specific terms in English that can be confusing for English learners (Echevarria, Vogt, & Short, 2010; NCTM, 2009). Further, what may be seen as lack of understanding of a process or operation could actually be the result of the student not understanding the teacher's explanation or instructions. In response to the question, "How do teachers sometimes make it difficult for you to learn?" one high school English learner replied, "For me, the hardest part was when they didn't give directions, and specifically in math because I know a lot of math but I didn't understand my teacher." Sometimes it is difficult to ascertain student knowledge and skill level when a communication gap exists.

Problematic social/emotional behaviors may be a result of frustration or embarrassment over an inability to understand others or to express oneself, especially in older learners. Many of the behaviors in this domain could result from cultural differences, unknown social cues, and unfamiliarity with subtle language such as what constitutes a joke or "teasing."

Nearly all the behaviors in the Attention domain overlap with characteristics of learning academic material in a second language. The cognitive and linguistic load for

English learners is significant and often manifests itself in ways such as difficulty maintaining attention and reluctance to engage in tasks that require sustained mental effort.

These cultural and linguistic factors must be considered as teams examine data about student performance and behavior. With more exposure to mainstream culture and English, learners will adjust to school expectations and improve academically. In contrast, English learners with learning disabilities will not make quick progress with exposure to English. Learning disabilities are life long and academic progress will be markedly slower than for a student whose only challenge is developing English proficiency. That said, individuals with learning disabilities can learn to compensate for areas of weakness, and with early, effective support, they can be highly successful and productive members of society. Figure 5.3 illustrates this point by showing a writing sample of a young adult with learning disabilities, who, despite her learning challenges—and obstacles she encountered throughout her schooling—has attained a masters degree and has been employed full time on the staff of a university for a number of years. As you can see, Candace continues to struggle with written language. For individuals like Candace, new research studies funded by the National Center for Technology Innovation are examining the usefulness of new assistive technologies such as spell-checking software designed for students with dyslexia, mobile tools for students with learning disabilities, and alternative Web browsers for students with visual disabilities. Further, the National Center for Learning Disabilities has a plethora of useful resources on the topic of learning disabilities, including free literacy and learning resources for Spanish-speaking families (http://getreadytoread.org).

Distinguishing Disability from Difference

We are often asked what is *the* way to tell if a child is struggling because of cultural and linguistic differences or if there is a learning disability and special education should be considered. First, with RTI, educators knowledgeable about second language issues and best practice are systematically adapting the learning environment, teaching methods, and materials to facilitate learning for each child. Special education should never be considered as the first option when students struggle.

Secondly, there is no single, specific assessment for determining disability with English learners. Accurate diagnosis requires careful examination of data by a multidisciplinary team. The composition of team membership is critical when considering the educational needs of English learners, especially if special education services are being contemplated. As mentioned throughout this book, individuals who have expertise in second language acquisition must be part of the decision-making process. In addition, professionals who are fluent in the student's language and are familiar with the student's and family's culture are valuable members of the team and provide essential information about the student's academic skills and behavior in both the home language and English. They can also interpret data in culturally and linguistically appropriate ways. The team should also include family and community members (and an interpreter), as well as the student, if age appropriate. Together, this type of team offers the best chance of examining data and accurately determining if the student's learning difficulties can be explained by sociocultural, linguistic, or learning variables (Salend & Salinas, 2003).

The data the team examines would include the following.

FIGURE 5.3 *Handwriting Sample*

I Just wanted to take a moment to say
Thank You vary much from The bottom of my
heart for taking the time to Lisan to my
concerns and strugals I vent Throuin my
first Year of my masters Programin Higher
EDucation. I have learned throu this exference
and Proven to my self most inportently that
I Deserve to Prusa my Goals in Higher
EDucation. I hnow you will take our talk
To heart and make improvements to The
Program for people with Disablitys and that
The next Person that walks in to this
Program will Not be Prusuaded out mearly
because they our just a little different/
SPetional. we all have to embras our
Dreams no matter what Negativity is
brought our way, esPetionaley in the filed
of higher ED. I Love this filed and
we just need to insure we nave The
best Profesors out helping US. Thanks
for giving me a voice!

Records. To the extent possible, look for cumulative files that will paint a picture of the child's educational history. In our own experience, there was a high school student who had not received any support over the years even though she read far below grade level. Her records indicated that she had been referred for special education assessment in second grade and her mother refused. Had anyone talked with the mother since? There may have been cultural implications for the mother's decision such as not understanding

completely what the school was recommending. Other important information would include how much primary language instruction the student has received, or if there has been adequate English language development provided. Also, the RTI forms provided in this book would be valuable documents that show the kinds of modifications and accommodations that were tried in general education as well as the type and duration of intervention the student received. Other records to examine are health records (Does the student need glasses or hearing aids?) and educational records from the home country, when possible.

Interviews. Families are our best informants and are not utilized often enough. At what age did the student begin talking? Has language development been normal? How much of the first language is used in the home? What are the literacy practices of the family? Does the family perceive that the child has difficulties? How does the child's development compare with that of siblings and peers? Has the child had any major health concerns or persistent illnesses? In addition to gathering interview data from family members, school staff such as the playground supervisor, cafeteria workers, and office staff may offer important insights about the student. Does the student appear to be a competent individual? Does she show strengths such as leadership qualities, interpersonal skills, etc.? Students may appear quite different outside of the classroom than during instructional time.

Observations. In-class observations are critical to determine if the student is being provided high-quality instruction that meets his or her needs. In Chapter 2 we discussed the impact of teacher attitude on achievement. What is the relationship between a teacher and students? Does the teacher hold high expectations for English learners, nurturing and supporting their language and academic development? How does the teacher promote interest and motivation? Are the students' background experiences tied to lessons? Also, as mentioned above, observation of behavior outside of the classroom provides a more complete picture of the student's strengths and areas of concern. Observations in the home are extremely informative, if home visits can be arranged.

Testing. Assessments provide valuable information on student academic performance. Coupled with the information discussed above, test results contribute to a comprehensive profile of a student's strengths and areas of difficulty. However, no single assessment should be used for placement into programs, nor should assessment results alone be considered, especially when making judgments about special education placement for English learners.

It bears repeating here that professional development opportunities for the entire staff (including general education and special education personnel) related to second language acquisition, effective instructional practice for English learners, and data collection and interpretation will strengthen the RTI process, particularly when looking for possible causes for an English learner's difficulty.

For a practitioner's perspective on the issue of diversity versus learning difficulty, in Figure 5.4 you can read the transcription of an interview with a teacher who taught for 20 years in a low-performing, predominantly low-income (95% free or reduced-price lunch) K–5 elementary school. Of the 1,651 students, 97% are Latino and 60% are English learners. Having been retired for less than a year at the time of the interview, Phil Giesen reflected on how he distinguished English language proficiency from a learning problem when so many of his students were functioning well below grade-level norms. Figure 5.5 shows the transcript of an interview with a former

FIGURE 5.4 *Distinguishing Disability from Difference: A Teacher's Experience*

At my school, almost all students were behind grade level. I always thought of the kids as just having different learning styles. I didn't think about referral to special education because it isn't a magic pill; it is my responsibility to reach the student. I had students read to me and I looked for some sort of pattern in their errors. Can they decode? If they are having problems with comprehension, maybe it is because they don't have strong skills in decoding. The ones who could read when they came from Mexico could transition pretty easily. But most students were born here so they couldn't read in Spanish and they can't read well in English because of the vocabulary. They can't self-correct since they haven't had enough exposure to English. So, if they pronounce knees as k-nees, they don't know to self-correct like an English speaker would.

One time I had two girls in class, Maria and Carmen, who had the same low English proficiency and low reading level. But, I suspected that Carmen had a learning disability by the way she read. I asked the special education teacher to observe them reading and she agreed with me that something more was going on with Carmen. How did we know? When Maria read aloud, she consistently struggled with decoding, made typical errors and seemed used to reading that way. When Carmen read, she seemed nervous, and read erratically, getting the same word right one time and wrong the next. Their English reading level was the same but it was the kind of errors that they made that made the two readers qualitatively different.

In another case, I had a boy in class who had been retained in second grade. In third grade Gilberto still couldn't read although he was around grade level in math. His family was poor, his mother spoke only Spanish, and Gilberto had developed some discipline issues, probably because of his reading problems. I worked with him on the basic components of reading—phonics, phonemic awareness, vocabulary, comprehension, etc. When he slowed down and focused he was able to make steady progress. By the end of the year, he was a reader! He made so much progress academically! Why hadn't he gotten the basics of reading before? Who knows? But with English learners, we start where they are and move them forward. I used whatever I could to get them to read. If they brought something into class, we'd use it as a teachable moment and discuss it, write about it and so forth. You have to use their experiences to engage them in learning.

Small group discussions helped detect if they had low English proficiency or if something else was going on. If they can't follow a discussion because of English proficiency, it is different than a processing problem. When you find a subject that interests a particular student, the EL student will usually persist in order to find alternative vocabulary words. I remember an incident when Luis (a 3rd grader) asked me during a discussion about whales if they were as big as the pyramids we had discussed a few weeks ago. His apparent ability to make this connection from different discussions reinforced my belief that he didn't have a processing problem.

Also, you should always check with the family to see if they notice a problem. One student had trouble expressing himself and had been referred to SST (student study team) and they thought he needed more English language development. I spoke with the mom and she said he was worse in Spanish. Family input is really important.

FIGURE 5.5 *A Special Educator's Perspective*

When I was a special education teacher, one of the teachers at my school always had 2 or 3 students from his class on the SST list. After a while, I got the impression that he wanted the team to refer kids for special education placement so they would be out of his class. (Now all students at the school are included in general education so his strategy wouldn't work!) One day I asked, "Does your credential say that you get to teach only the easy kids? Because mine says I have to teach ALL kids." He got the point. Some teachers think that if a student has learning or behavior challenges then they should be in special education. The reality is that, at best, they will receive more support for part of the day but they will still be a part of the general education classroom. I had an English learner who could fully participate in class discussions, but he couldn't read or write. There are things we can do to support these kids' access to text like using a laptop with software that lets him dictate instead of writing or providing books on tape.

special education teacher at the same school. These practitioners' perspectives are intended to show how one might meet the needs of English learners and support their learning.

In sum, to distinguish between language differences and learning disabilities, keep in mind that learning disabilities will be manifested in a variety of ways in school and in life, regardless of the language students speak. A student cannot have a learning disability just in English and not in his or her home language. Therefore, some overarching questions to ask about English learners include:

Does the student differ significantly from others with similar background?

Does his or her family see a problem?

What about first language development? Was it normal?

Does the difficulty the student is experiencing result primarily from cultural, environmental, or economic disadvantage?

Is the student making steady progress, regardless how slow?

Has the student had an opportunity to demonstrate knowledge and skills in his or her home language?

Has the student had sufficient opportunities to learn by hearing engaging stories, reading interesting texts, and using the home language for literacy development and background information?

The answers to these questions are essential for identifying the source of a student's difficulty in the classroom.

Successful IEP Meetings

One critical factor in conducting effective IEP meetings begins with the kind of services that are offered at the school. Service providers working with culturally and linguistically diverse students such as the general education teachers, school counselor, speech/language therapist, and occupational therapist need to have the same knowledge base, philosophy, and practice when working with English learners. Services should be coordinated among these professionals and they should use culturally responsive approaches to serving English learners.

Another factor is engaging parents in the process. In order to gain the critical support of and cooperation needed from parents, we should make sure that they are informed partners who are included in the IEP process. They are your best informants about the student. Some suggestions for involving parents of English learners in IEP meetings include (Cardenes-Hagan, 2007):

- Reassure the parents that you are all there to help.
- Have an interpreter available at the meeting.
- Take meetings step by step, making sure parents understand everything being discussed.
- Suggest what parents can do at home to help.

FIGURE 5.6 *Guide to Effective RTI Implementation: Tier 3*

Who Is Responsible?	
Modification(s) and/or Intervention(s)	
Length of Time	
Teacher-Pupil Ratio	
Assessments Needed	
Assessments Used	
Frequency of Progress Monitoring	
Treatment Fidelity Observation	
Review of Modification(s) and/or Intervention(s)	

FIGURE 5.6 *Continued*

Necessary Professional Development (For whom and by whom)	
Parent Involvement	
Forms/Resources	

- Offer an open-door policy, with an invitation for questions and frequent communication.
- Offer a list of community resources.

In addition to community resources, there are a host of resources available online as well. The National Center for Learning Disabilities (www.ncld.org) recommends that parents know their rights so that they are more confident during meetings, and that parents should trust their own instincts because they have a unique perspective. They are able to highlight their child's capabilities and talents, which helps education professionals see the student as a whole person—not just someone with a learning disability. A parent guide is found at http://www.ncld.org/publications-a-more/parent-advocacy-guides/idea-parent-guide. Other resources include www.LDOnLine.org and Colorín Colorado (www.ColorinColorado .org, section on learning disabilities). These sorts of resources should be provided to parents so that they are more apt to participate in and be comfortable with the often daunting nature of formal IEP meetings.

Finally, the team must recommend a program for the student that meets his or her needs—culturally, linguistically, academically, and/or behaviorally. The IEP document may specify the extent to which primary language instruction will be provided, as well as the amount of explicit English language development (including oral language development) the student will receive each day. Other features of a culturally and linguistically appropriate IEP may, for example, specify practices such as explicitly teaching the connections (similarities and differences) between the home language and English, and specific use of a student's background experiences to make text meaningful and improve comprehension.

Final Thoughts

One of the most perplexing issues in working with struggling English learners is disentangling language from learning problems. English learners will not outgrow true learning disabilities. However, as English learners acquire more English proficiency, experience

high-quality instruction, and learn the expectations of school and society, their perform-ance will change over time.

English learners receiving Tier 3 intervention have been taught using effective in-struction in Tier 1 and classroom modification and accommodations have been docu-mented. They further participated in Tier 2 intervention in which progress was carefully monitored and documented. Tier 3 intervention offers students an opportunity to receive even more intensive instruction that focuses on their specific needs, is provided more fre-quently, for longer duration, and is implemented by a highly trained teacher. Progress is monitored weekly. As a result of these efforts, the careful observation and documentation of performance throughout the RTI process will assist educators in distinguishing lan-guage differences from learning disabilities.

For Reflection and Discussion

1. Use your Guide to Effective RTI Implementation (Figure 5.6) to determine what might be considered some of the most critical issues to examine at Tier 3.

2. Characteristics of learning disabilities and those of learning a new language overlap to a degree. How would you explain to your colleagues ways to differentiate between the two?

3. Read through the profiles presented at the beginning of the chapter. Which type of student is most common in your school? What specific information in this chapter most applies to your students?

4. Why is it essential to distinguish between a language acquisition issue and learning problems at Tier 3?

Special Considerations for Secondary English Learners

What RTI does is put everybody on the same playing field. It doesn't matter what your language structure is, whether or not you're disabled, or whether or not you're poor. What matters is that you need to progress at a satisfactory pace in the general curriculum.

Wayne Sailor, University of Kansas; as reported in Duffy, n.d.

Although the initial focus of RTI was on the elementary grades, particularly grades K–3, many districts are now extending RTI through grade 12. While we must provide intervention as soon as possible for young children, it is of equal importance to provide intensive support, both academically and behaviorally, for middle, junior, and high school students. In reality, the stakes are even greater for adolescents who lack the necessary knowledge and skills to successfully negotiate secondary curriculums because they are at-risk for dropping out of school. The need for intervention at the secondary level is clearly evident, as indicated by the following statistics:

- According to the National Assessment of Educational Progress (NAEP), approximately two-thirds of students in grades eight through twelve read at less than a "proficient" level (Rampey, Dion, & Donahue, 2009).

- Approximately 40% of high school graduates lack the literacy skills that employers seek (Short & Fitzsimmons, 2006).

- Only 30% of all secondary students read proficiently, but for students of color, the situation is worse: 89% of Hispanic students and 86% of African American middle and high school students read below grade level (Perie, Grigg, & Donahue, 2005).

- A lingering divide in achievement exists between Caucasian students and those from linguistically and culturally diverse groups (Echevarria, Vogt, & Short, 2010b). On the 2008 National Assessment of Educational Progress (NAEP), compared to 2004, there was no significant change in the gap in reading scores between White and Hispanic students at age 17. However, the gap between White and Hispanic 17-year-olds in 2008 narrowed by 15 points compared to 1975 (NAEP, 2008). (As of this writing, the results of the 2009 NAEP have not been reported.)

- Since the No Child Left Behind Act (NCLB) has been implemented, there appears to have been an increase in the number of high school English learners not receiving a diploma because they failed high-stakes tests, despite fulfilling all other graduate requirements (Biancarosa & Snow, 2004).

In this chapter, we focus on language, literacy, and academic development for adolescent English learners, including issues of assessment and screening, curriculum and its relevancy to adolescents, scheduling, and professional development. In addition, we examine differences in RTI that are unique to English learners at the secondary level (grades 6–12). Finally, we offer recommendations and direction for implementing RTI for English learners in middle, junior, and high schools.

Literacy Issues for Secondary English Learners

As we begin, it's important to consider the language and academic development needs of adolescent English learners, including the approximately 56% who are native-born (Capps, et al., 2005). Many of these students, who have been schooled exclusively in the United States, are lacking sufficient proficiency in English to enable them to succeed academically. For a number of reasons, these English learners have become "stalled," meaning that they plateau at the intermediate level of English proficiency. This is insufficient for academic success at the secondary level.

For these adolescents, "prevention," a frequently used term in the elementary grades and in RTI, may seem to be an odd choice of words. By the time many of these students reach middle school, they already have a history of academic failure that usually becomes worse once they attend high school. However, because literacy is a key to academic success in the secondary grades, students who are poor readers and writers are quite likely to perform poorly in high school academic subjects (Ehren, n.d.). By continuing to develop English language proficiency, and by targeting reading, writing, listening, and speaking skills, these same students are more likely to avoid comprehensive school failure.

There are a number of factors impacting adolescent literacy development, for both native speakers and English learners alike. We know that successful readers need much more than adequate decoding skills and the ability to read words correctly and quickly (Brozo, 2010). Students at the secondary level also must be able to use a wide variety of sophisticated reading strategies flexibly and purposefully. They must see themselves as successful, able, and authorized members of learning communities (Sturtevant, et al., 2006). If all secondary students are expected to develop sophisticated levels of reading and writing, as well as self-realization, why are so many struggling to meet this universal goal?

Why Do Secondary English Learners Struggle with Reading and Writing?

Adolescent English learners have reading and writing problems in middle, junior, and high school classrooms for some of the following reasons:

- At the secondary level, there is a strong relationship between literacy proficiency and academic achievement because of the need for students to master academic English. For example, students must use English to read and understand complex expository prose found in textbooks and reference materials, write persuasively, argue and support points of view, take notes from lectures or the Internet, articulate their thinking, generate hypotheses and predictions, express analyses, draw conclusions, and so forth. They must use their emerging English knowledge along with content knowledge to complete assigned tasks. These three knowledge bases—knowledge of English, knowledge of content, and knowledge of how tasks are to be accomplished, constitute the major elements of academic literacy (Echevarria, Vogt, & Short, 2010b; Short, 2002). In many classrooms where English learners are present, secondary content teachers do not attend to teaching academic literacy within their subject matter curriculums (Short & Fitzsimmons, 2006).

- In classrooms where teachers embed literacy practices in their subject area instruction, the lessons are often mediated by students' expectations and responses to them, and teachers adjust accordingly, perhaps by changing or omitting the literacy-related assignments when students respond negatively to them (O'Brien, Stewart, & Moje, 1995; Vogt, 1989). Students have their own ideas about what constitutes learning in a subject area classroom and teachers make decisions about teaching practices in conjunction with their students and the culture of secondary schools (Moje, 1996).

- Many schools fail to align their curricula with student interests and out-of-school competencies. Many secondary students who are unwilling to engage in school literacy practices actively engage in out-of-school literacy practices that they believe are important and powerful. Think about your students' use of networking websites such

as Facebook, blogs, and Twitter. Each of these requires a relatively sophisticated level of literacy (reading and writing), yet these modes of communication aren't generally considered valid examples of "school writing" (Moje, 2008; Tatum, 2008).

- Many secondary schools do not value an additive literacy curriculum that builds on and further develops English learners' native language literacy skills (Bauer, 2009).

- Literacy development is especially challenging for English learners who enter the U.S. educational system in the secondary grades, not only because of the complex course content but also because these students have fewer years to learn English (Short & Fitzsimmons, 2006).

- The sheer number of secondary students needing reading assistance is disproportionate to the number of support personnel, such as reading specialists, who are available to provide needed intensive instruction.

- The configuration of secondary schools with multiple classroom periods and a variety of teachers results in no one "owning" a student academically, as contrasted with elementary, self-contained classrooms with one teacher. Therefore, students with literacy problems can more easily slip through the cracks until they are experiencing difficulty in or are failing several classes. High school counselors, generally responsible for overseeing many students, are often notified only after a particular student has experienced academic distress or failure.

- Most English learners with intermediate or early advanced proficiency no longer receive intensive English language instruction. Many English learners, including newcomer students, receive little to no ELD or ESL instruction at the secondary level (Gedney, 2009).

- There is a wide range of academic and English proficiency levels in any given secondary classroom. Some adolescent English learners have below grade-level literacy skills in their native language (L1), while others are exceptionally literate in their L1, but struggle to read and write in English. Similarly, some immigrant English learners have had consistent, effective schooling experiences prior to coming to the United States. Others have had interrupted and ineffective schooling, while still others have a background of little or no schooling. Immigrant English learners are also more likely to be poor than non-immigrants (Batalova, Fix, & Murray, 2005). Considering English learners as students who all need the same type of instruction makes no more sense than teaching native speakers exclusively in a whole class configuration, with no attempts at differentiation.

- Many secondary teachers report they are unprepared to meet the language, literacy, and academic needs of their students who are English learners (Echevarria, Vogt, & Short, 2010b; Short & Fitzsimmons, 2006). Therefore, it is not surprising that in recent years English learners have been both over- and under-identified for special education services, resulting in inappropriate placements for many.

- Researchers in the literacy field are advocating the teaching of 21st-century literacy skills to all secondary students in order to prepare them for the technological work of the future (Ajayi, 2009; Black, 2009; Moje, 2008; Sox & Rubenstein-Ávila, 2009; Vogt & Shearer, 2011). This finding has huge implications for how secondary literacy programs are designed, including the texts, materials, and methods that are used for classroom instruction and intervention.

- Literacy educators have been concerned for many years about students' motivation to engage in literacy activities, because a lack of motivation negatively impacts reading development. We know that there is a decline in motivation to read as students become older, and older adolescent males are less motivated to read than younger adolescent males (Pitcher, et al., 2007). With native-speaking adolescents, a lack of motivation may be manifested as apathy and frustration. Given different topics and materials, these same students may exhibit high motivation. The issue for English learners is that many may be very motivated to read (see Sturtevant & Kim, 2010), but their lack of English proficiency may be perceived as a lack of motivation.

- As with elementary teachers, another major issue for secondary teachers is how to appropriately assess an English learner's literacy and academic strengths and needs, both in English and in the student's home language. It is very challenging for a secondary content teacher to determine whether an English learner's difficulties in class are due to a language proficiency issue, a reading problem, incomplete or insufficient background knowledge about a topic, or limited knowledge of the academic language and vocabulary needed for comprehending the content concepts (Echevarria, Vogt, & Short, 2010b).

According to Short and Fitzsimmons (2006, p. 14), the major challenges to improving the literacy of adolescent English learners can be summarized as follows:

1. Lack of common criteria for identifying English learners and tracking their academic performance;

2. Lack of appropriate assessments for measuring native-language literacy, content knowledge, and English literacy development;

3. Inadequate educator capacity for improving literacy in adolescent English learners;

4. Lack of appropriate and flexible program options;

5. Inadequate use of research-based instructional practices;

6. Lack of a strong and coherent research agenda about adolescent English learner literacy. (See Short & Fitzsimmons, 2006, for a comprehensive discussion of each of these challenges.)

All of the issues listed in this section have implications for how secondary educators create and implement an effective and appropriate plan for RTI. Not surprisingly, while some RTI elements are the same for both elementary and secondary classrooms, there are also substantial differences that must be considered when designing a secondary RTI program for English learners.

Implementation of RTI for English Learners at the Secondary Level

Although research around RTI at the elementary level has been ongoing, studies looking into the best ways of implementing the process for secondary students are scant . . . [In] the absence of research and documented successes at the secondary level it falls to middle and high schools to devise their own approaches to implementing

responsive tiered interventions for adolescent literacy. This is ironic because the provision in IDEA stresses the need for RTI programs to be supported by interventions that are based on scientific research . . . (Brozo, 2010, p. 278)

As stated above, we have few research findings to guide us toward effective implementation of RTI at the secondary level. However, we do know that key differences exist between implementing RTI at the elementary and secondary levels. Some of these differences include the following (Pennsylvania Department of Education, 2008, p. 19):

- There are fewer models about how to implement RTI at the secondary level.
- Students from multiple feeder schools enter into the secondary schools.
- There is a much higher student–teacher ratio in the secondary grades.
- Teachers are content specialists, and many do not have the training to know how to help students who lack language and literacy skills and strategies.
- There is an increased focus in many secondary schools on knowledge dissemination rather than independent skill acquisition and development.
- Student expectations include independent self-monitoring, organization, self-motivation, and increased responsibility for learning.
- Students' non-school responsibilities are many, and include employment, family responsibilities, driving, and dating.
- There are fewer structures in place in secondary schools to foster parent involvement.

Even if we do not have research-based recommendations for designing secondary RTI programs, there are substantial research findings and recommendations about what constitutes effective literacy instruction for adolescents. In the next section, we examine these recommendations within the context of the needs of diverse English learners.

What Adolescent English Learners Need and Deserve: Effective Tier 1 Instruction

During the past decade, there have been a number of important initiatives calling for reform in adolescent literacy instruction. Concerns about poor adolescent literacy achievement have generated funding from the federal government and private agencies and organizations, with the goal of increasing the reading and writing abilities of adolescents. Some of the major initiatives include: Time to Act, 2009, the largest ever research endeavor related to adolescent literacy, funded by the Carnegie Institute; Reading Next: A Vision for Research in Middle and High School Literacy (Biancarosa & Snow, 2004), with fifteen essential elements for improving adolescent literacy instruction; and Race to the Top, 2009, which provides grants from stimulus funds for K–12, with a focus on college or workforce preparedness for adolescents. In addition, the two largest professional literacy organizations, the International Reading Association (IRA), and the National Council of Teachers of English (NCTE), have each published position papers on the timely topic of adolescent literacy (see www.reading.org and www.ncte.org).

FIGURE 6.1 *Program Checklist for Middle, Junior, and High School Literacy Programs*

To what degree do the following elements exist within your secondary school program?

1. A literacy program based on school-wide needs assessment data

2. A long-range literacy plan (two to three years) with systematic, focused evaluation of progress toward meeting stated goals

3. Adequate time for literacy instruction at all grade levels, 6–12

4. A school-wide commitment to literacy practices implemented by content area teachers and embedded in high-quality instruction across the curriculum

5. Use of both formative and summative assessment to drive instruction and to evaluate implementation

6. A commitment to understanding and implementing principled practices in literacy instruction, by incorporating those practices with reading, writing, speaking, and listening

7. Strong literacy leadership by knowledgeable and committed administrators

8. Allocation of adequate resources, materials, personnel, and other needed support for literacy

9. Commitment to hiring an adequate number of highly qualified coaches and reading and math specialists, and other specialists to support teachers and students in innovative and substantive ways

10. Adequate and sustained support for readers with diverse abilities and specific language and literacy needs, and the teachers who interact with them

11. Adequate support for technology as well as a school-wide commitment to understanding the needs of students and teachers in the use of technology

12. Opportunities for teachers to engage in collaborative efforts to inform, promote, and improve literacy practice within the school

13. Support for individual and school-wide sustained professional development driven by data from the needs assessment

14. Commitment to creating a literacy program that is culturally responsive to the context of the community and incorporates an active parent and community voice in educational decisions

Source: Adapted from Vogt & Shearer, 2011.

Recommendations from these initiatives and documents are remarkably similar and they are summarized in the next section. We hope these recommendations, including the added considerations for English learners, and the checklist in Figure 6.1 will be helpful as you plan your Tier 1 classroom instruction for secondary English learners.

Eight Principles of Adolescent Literacy Instruction (adapted from Vogt & Shearer, 2011)

1. **Adolescents need an assessment-based literacy program of comprehension instruction embedded in rich content that values peer mediation for comprehension, discussion, collaboration, and social learning.** From research (Shearer, Ruddell, & Vogt, 2001), we learned that students with reading problems can read challenging texts given support and instruction in how to: (1) read multisyllabic words; and (2) engage in meaningful discussions that challenge them to support positions and argue points of view. Mr. Gonzalez, a secondary teacher, provides his students with many opportunities to practice and improve their academic English through reading texts that are sometimes adapted to meet their proficiency levels. He has taught his students how to engage in instructional conversations (see Echevarria,

Vogt, & Short, 2010b) and refers frequently to classroom posters that list "signal words" (see Vogt & Echevarria, 2008) that enable English learners to use academic vocabulary during discussion and in writing. Mr. Gonzalez's comprehension instruction focuses on developing a variety of learning strategies, as well as exploring differences in how readers comprehend narrative, expository, and informational texts. His assessment of student comprehension is ongoing and continuous, using both informal (e.g., observation, spot-checks, group response) and formal methods (tests, writing assignments, diagnostic assessments).

2. **Adolescents need explicit instruction in domain-specific literacy practices, and critical literacy provided in their content area classrooms to prepare them for college and employment.** Domain-specific literacy practices include learning the academic language and vocabulary of the disciplines (e.g., history/social studies, the sciences, literature, and so forth); and critical literacy practices require readers to question author assumptions and biases, check evidence for factual information, and provide counterpoint arguments, as needed. In his classroom, Mr. Gonzalez teaches his English learners and other students to be critical consumers of what they read, whether in print or electronically. For example, his students examine issues of perspective in the local newspaper's opinion page, on television newscasts, and in publications such as *Time, Newsweek*, and the *Wall Street Journal*. In order for his English learners to be successful with these critical literacy tasks, Mr. Gonzalez encourages them to work with partners and small groups, and he provides a variety of scaffolds to support their learning (e.g., as tape recorded articles, marginal notes, and highlighted texts).

3. **Adolescents need to consume and produce a wide variety of rich text materials across genres and literacies.** They need classroom instruction that recognizes the benefits of using reading and writing as a means to enhance learning in the content areas and in everyday communication, in work and in recreation. Mr. Gonzalez carefully plans lessons that include a variety of texts, genres, and tasks that require students to read, write, converse, and listen during each period.

4. **Adolescents need a curriculum that honors students' sociocultural contexts and language foundations, capitalizes on individuals' diverse funds of knowledge, and provides literacy support for successful learning.** Mr. Gonzalez builds on the experiential and knowledge-based learning of his students through activities that promote activation of prior knowledge and that develop background knowledge where gaps exist. For example, he occasionally permits English learners to complete a quick-write activity in their primary language, and orally share the writing in their L1 with other students who speak the same language. Obviously, Mr. Gonzalez doesn't speak all of the home languages of his students, but he is able to assess quickly whether his students have background knowledge in a particular topic by watching them write and share their information. Too often, teachers think English learners "lack background knowledge," when in reality, the students are unable to share what they know and have experienced in English. When given the opportunity to share their knowledge and experiences in their home language, formerly quiet, disengaged students become more engaged. If it's possible to have another student orally explain or interpret the quick-write in English, the writer's thoughts and background knowledge can be further validated.

5. **Adolescents need rich, engaging, motivating instruction. They need opportunities for self-directed learning and the ability to set achievable goals that promote efficacy.** Mr. Gonzalez values self-directed small group and partner work in his classrooms. He also knows that adolescents are more motivated to carry out their own rather than the teacher's goals. Although he posts and orally explains his content and language objectives for each lesson, he also encourages his students to write their own personal learning and language goals, especially when beginning a new unit. Mr. Gonzalez frequently permits student choice of projects, independent research, and even reading material (print and electronic). He has found that when adolescents are given choices and then are provided with scaffolds to enable them to be successful, they can and will complete challenging tasks.

6. **Adolescents need vocabulary instruction that is explicit, contextualized, and that targets strategies that promote independent vocabulary acquisition.** Note the words "explicit" and "contextualized." Mr. Gonzalez uses a variety of techniques for bringing more context into the teaching of academic vocabulary. These include activities like Four Corners Vocabulary Charts (Vogt & Echevarria, 2008), embedding definitions of key vocabulary into sentences that introduce the words, repetition and review of key vocabulary throughout and across lessons, and explicit teaching of fewer (rather than more) words. When selecting vocabulary, he focuses on words that are key to understanding a lesson's content, words that involve language processes and functions that students will be engaged in (e.g., summarize, compare and contrast, generate questions), and words that enable ongoing learning of new vocabulary (e.g., words with the same root: *photo*copy, *photo*graphy, *photo*synthesis) (Echevarria, Vogt, & Short, 2008; 2010a; 2010b).

7. **Adolescents need instruction in technologies that facilitate their ability to use new forms of in-school and out-of-school literacy practices.** Mr. Gonzalez strives for relevancy in his teaching and one way to be relevant to his students is to honor and expand their use of technology resources. In a lesson that explored perspective and persuasive writing techniques, students were expected to blog about particular topics, read each other's blogs, and analyze how the choice of words and phrases can influence and convince. The students then read some historic speeches they found on the Internet and identified the words and phrases used to persuade and influence.

8. **Adolescents benefit from differentiated instruction and intensity of support based on individual needs that are linked to assessment, and are implemented in grouping configurations that range from partners to whole class.** Secondary students need opportunities to explore ideas individually and to engage collaboratively in project learning. This leads to differentiated instruction, which is at the heart of effective RTI, whatever the tier or intervention. Mr. Gonzalez frequently differentiates classroom tasks, processes, and products according to his students' language proficiency and assessed needs. For example, in one multi-period lesson, he asked a few students to do independent research in several texts and articles he brought to class. This information was shared with another group who used it to write and perform a skit modeled after a newscast with interviews. Other students with less English proficiency worked with Mr. Gonzalez on an Internet search and together they summarized their findings and presented them to the class in writing. The teacher differentiates in

other ways, too, including working with small groups of students to pre-teach a lesson's key concepts and vocabulary, or re-teach a lesson for students needing additional support.

Following are some additional principles for adolescent English learners (adapted from Short & Fitzsimmons, 2007):

- Integrate all four language skills (reading, writing, listening, speaking) from the start, regardless of student proficiency (Genesee, et al., 2006).
- Include multiple opportunities for oral language practice because it facilitates English literacy development (August & Shanahan, 2006).
- Teach the components and processes of reading and writing, explicitly and as needed according to literacy assessment findings.
- Teach reading and other learning strategies explicitly and provide practice and scaffolding for transfer from L1 strategy use (Riches & Genesee, 2006).
- Teach language, when possible, through content and themes related to real-life experiences.

As with elementary Tier 1 instruction, we advocate that secondary content teachers who have English learners in their classroom, become highly qualified SIOP® teachers (see Chapter 1). Because the SIOP® Model is curriculum and materials neutral (that is, any content, curriculum, and/or materials can be used by SIOP® teachers), the principles and recommendations previously listed are compatible with high-quality implementation of the SIOP® Model (Echevarria, Vogt, & Short, 2010b).

When creating appropriate classroom instruction for English learners (and all other students), remember the following words of literacy expert Bill Brozo:

> RTI at the secondary level is only as good as its preventive supports. If content teachers fail to offer responsive literacy instruction to benefit every student and differentiated assistance for those in need of extra help, then the preventive potential of RTI is lost. When this happens, RTI at the secondary level becomes little more than a delivery system for remedial reading and, as such, cannot be regarded as a comprehensive program that supports the literacy competencies of all youth. (2010, p. 280)

What Adolescent English Learners Need and Deserve: Effective Tier 2 and Tier 3 Instruction

Without a doubt, adolescent English learners will benefit from the Tier 2 and Tier 3 recommendations included in Chapters 4 and 5. However, once again, there are unique considerations for designing and implementing more intensive RTI interventions at the middle, junior, and high school levels. These include the following:

1. Consider both in-school and out-of-school literacies when designing interventions for adolescent English learners. Their out-of-school literacies, including

Internet searches, social networking sites, WebQuests, online fan fiction, hobbies, computer games, and so forth, can provide a gateway to in-school literacy instruction.

2. Many adolescent English learners have also developed a wide range of household literacy skills while helping their parents and other family members negotiate with doctors, school personnel, retail outlets, and public agencies. Others hold part-time jobs in which they regularly develop and use literacy-related skills. These out-of-school literacy skills can serve as a bridge to in-school literacy instruction.

3. Motivation, identity, choice, and engagement are important factors for all adolescents, including English learners. Tier 2 and 3 interventions for adolescents should include guided, self-selection of reading materials, a focus on English morphology and multi-syllabic words, and vocabulary self-selection (see Ruddell, 2007; Shearer, Ruddell, & Vogt, 2001, for a thorough description and discussion of each of these elements).

4. One of the biggest challenges at the secondary level is the master schedule that generally requires a semester-long commitment to a class. Therefore, a number of options need to be considered for Tier 2 interventions to assist students in meeting graduation requirements. Some possibilities include (National Center for Learning Disabilities, 2008):

   a. Offer an intensive learning strategies course for credit.

   b. Create summer school "bridge" programs to help students transition from elementary to middle school, and middle school to high school.

   c. Offer before- and after-school intervention programs; when considering this option, however, remember issues such as busing. A lack of transportation between school and home can sabotage even the most promising intervention program, as evidenced by a situation encountered by one of the authors (MaryEllen) who created a middle school intensive reading intervention with 90+ students who were referred by their teachers. The intervention teachers were trained and materials were purchased for the in-school class. Because of scheduling issues, the intervention class was moved to after school. However, only one student was able to attend because the other students had transportation problems.

   d. Offer a "class" within a class. This option is possible within a middle school block schedule for Language Arts, especially if an instructional aide is available to monitor and assist the other students.

   e. Recommend extended graduation, allowing five years for students who need more time.

   f. Examine intervention models that are effective across content areas. Age- and developmentally appropriate interventions that work for adolescents in all subject areas prompt more buy-in from teachers for RTI.

   g. Examine the need, when working with secondary adolescents, to put additional behavioral interventions in place, such as mentoring, peer support programs, and systems to reward positive behaviors through incentives and structured advisories (Pennsylvania Department of Education, 2008).

Secondary RTI for English Learners: Putting It All Together

In this final section, we examine four options for organizing a secondary RTI program for English learners. The first suggests a five-tiered approach to meeting individual students' literacy and academic needs with increasing levels of intensity (see Figure 6.2). Please note that we do not intend to imply that students should be tracked throughout the school day in a particular level. For far too many years, adolescents have been consigned to academic tracks that were deleterious to all but the highest achieving students (see Oakes, 1985), and the practice continues today. Instead, in line with RTI and SIOP® principles that decry fixed ability groups for instruction, these options provide for flexibility, depending on a student's language, literacy, behavioral, and academic needs. The amount of time needed in each level or tier should be determined by in-depth assessment and consistent, effective progress monitoring.

The Pennsylvania Department of Education (2008) has been in the forefront of providing its educators with guidelines and recommendations for implementing RTI programs, including those at the secondary level. We have adapted these guidelines for English learners and, depending on your context, we believe that any one of these options can be viable for middle and high schools where English learners are present (see Figure 6.3). Our primary adaptations are the addition of the SIOP® Model instruction for all Tier 1 teachers of

FIGURE 6.2 *Secondary RTI Option 1 for English Learners*

Level 1: Enhanced Content Instruction with the SIOP® Model	Use of instructional methods in core content subjects that develop language, literacy, and content proficiency for all students, regardless of literacy levels, and that provides students the competitive skills they need for post-graduate success.
Level 2: Embedded Strategy Instruction	Use of instructional methods in and across content classes that provide practice in the use of learning strategies in whole-class configurations that allow access to college-ready curriculum.
Level 3: Intensive Strategy Instruction	Use of instructional methods that develop mastery of specific learning strategies for students needing short-term instruction of the strategies embedded throughout classroom lessons.
Level 4: Intensive Basic Skill Instruction	Use of instructional methods that develop mastery of entry-level language and literacy skills for students needing intensive, accelerated language and literacy intervention.
Level 5: Therapeutic Intervention	Use of instructional methods that develop mastery of language and literacy foundations related to the content and learning strategies that occur in classroom instruction for language-disabled students.

Source: Adapted from Lenz, Ehren, & Deshler, 2005.

chapter 6 / Special Considerations for Secondary English Learners

FIGURE 6.3 *Secondary RTI Options 2, 3, 4 for English Learners*

Option 2	Option 3	Option 4
ELD/ESL, depending on students' English proficiency.	ELD/ESL, depending on students' English proficiency.	ELD/ESL, depending on student's English proficiency.
Tier 1 and 2 students receive grade-level instruction in heterogeneous classes.	Tier 1 and 2 students receive grade-level instruction in heterogeneous classes.	All language arts classes are homogenously grouped in two-period blocks.
Tier 2 students receive an extra period of strategic intervention.	Tier 2 students receive an extra period of strategic intervention in homogeneous classes.	Tier 1 and 2 students receive grade-level instruction plus an extra period for enrichment or strategic instruction.
Students receive Tier 3 interventions for two periods.	Tier 3 students receive two periods of intensive instruction that is either in addition to or replaces the core and an elective class.	Tier 3 students receive two periods of intensive intervention that is either in addition to or replaces grade-level instruction and an elective class. Classes are parallel scheduled to allow student movement based on data.
Classes occur throughout the day.	Reading/language arts classes are parallel scheduled.	

Source: Adapted from the Pennsylvania Department of Education, 2008, p. 11.

English learners (and ideally for all intervention providers), and English language development (ELD or ESL), depending on students' English proficiency needs. You will find a wealth of information about RTI and other initiatives at the Pennsylvania Department of Education website for the Pennsylvania Training and Technical Assistance Network (www.pattan.net).

Final Thoughts

Interviewer:

> *"If you could tell teachers one thing to do that would help you learn more easily, what would it be?"*

High school English learners:

> *"I'd say, 'Be patient.'"*
>
> *"Don't just talk to the kids who know English. Talk to us, too."*
>
> *"Show us what we're supposed to do in the order we have to do it."*

"When we get to work in a group, we can learn from each other and practice our English."

"My math teacher just talks loud. I hear him fine . . . I just don't know what he's saying."

"Explain things to us so we understand them. Draw pictures, say things over again, show us things—do <u>anything</u> you can to help us understand."

"Don't forget we're here."

(Interviewed and videotaped at public high schools in Reno, NV and Boise, ID)

After reading numerous publications with countless recommendations about what RTI for secondary schools should include, we realized that not one of the suggestions came from those who matter the most: the students. When asked, adolescent English learners will respond with pinpoint clarity about what their teachers need to do to help them be effective. Similarly, they can quickly identify exactly what teachers do to make their job as students very challenging. As Allington states (2008, p. 1), "Most struggling readers never catch up with their higher-achieving classmates because schools create school days for them where they struggle all day long." For these students, English learners and native speakers alike, the SIOP® Model offers the best chance for them to receive the instruction in content and language that they need to make academic progress toward meeting rigorous content standards. For those who need more, effective RTI instruction in Tiers 2 and 3, with English language support, provides the last chance for many to achieve high school graduation.

For Reflection and Discussion

1. Many screening instruments and other assessments used at the elementary levels (and discussed in earlier chapters) are also appropriate for secondary students, but perhaps not for English learners. What assessment information do you need to gather to adequately assess English learners' language and academic strengths and needs?

2. There are few, if any, assessments that screen adolescents' out-of-school literacies. Consider your secondary student population, and the types of literacy activities these students engage in outside of school. What survey questions could you ask to elicit helpful information about these literacies, and how might the information you gather influence the development of your secondary RTI program?

3. As you consider the recommendations from this chapter, which are relevant to and doable for your present secondary school configuration? Consider your school's master schedule, staffing, support personnel, curriculum initiatives, and so forth. Which of the recommendations would require some systemic changes for your school?

4. As you read about Mr. Gonzalez's classroom approaches, you may have noticed that we never identified his subject area specialty or grade level. As you read, did you think he is an English teacher? Or Math, Science, or History? Is he a middle school or high school teacher? Does it make a difference? For English learners (and struggling readers), it is important that all secondary teachers, regardless of content area and grade level, adhere to the literacy principles as often as possible if these students are to make academic gains.

chapter 7

Successes and Barriers to Effective RTI Implementation

RTI is intended to function as a schoolwide approach for maximizing student outcomes and minimizing the number of students who eventually are labeled as "disabled." As such, there are a number of elements that contribute to a well-orchestrated process among staff, parents, and students. Fuchs and Deshler (2007) suggest the following elements for effective RTI implementation:

1. Significant and sustained investment in professional development to provide teachers with the array of skills they need to implement RTI and a system for addressing ongoing staff turnover.

2. Engaged administrators who set expectations for RTI implementation, provide the necessary resources, and support the use of procedures that ensure fidelity of implementation.

3. District-level support to hire teachers who not only embrace RTI principles but also have the prerequisite skills to implement them well in their classrooms.

4. A willingness of staff (teachers, specialists, school psychologists) to have their roles redefined in ways that support effective implementation.

5. The degree to which staff is given sufficient time to "make sense of" and put RTI into their instructional practice.

6. The extent of grassroots buy-in and participation in decision-making regarding the adoption of RTI.

These elements also apply to RTI for English learners, yet each has a specific overlay that is pertinent to English learners. Professional development also must include an understanding of the needs of English learners, knowledge about second language acquisition, and knowledge of research-based practices for this population. It is essential that administrators be familiar with best practice for English learners to ensure high-quality instruction and intervention in the RTI process. New hires should have a background in working effectively with culturally and linguistically diverse students and be committed to supporting them for academic success. Redefinition of roles may include working collaboratively with the ESL specialist or bilingual personnel, breaking down the territoriality that often exists among professionals in schools. Not only does it take time to understand and implement RTI, but changing instructional practice to meet the needs of English learners within RTI is a not an easy or quick process. Changing teacher practice requires significant time and ongoing support (Saunders, Goldenberg, & Gallimore, 2009), and both would be necessary for most teachers to reach a level of comfort that allows the best practices outlined in Chapter 3 to become routine and automatic. Finally, all staff need to have a voice in the development and implementation of RTI, including bilingual and ESL personnel.

Principles of a Successful RTI Program

There are various guiding principles for districts to follow, many of which are mentioned throughout this book. The International Reading Association's RTI Commission has identified six guiding principles for Response to Intervention (International Reading Association,

February/March, 2010, p. 1). Additional information about each of these principles can be found at www.reading.org. The RTI Guiding Principles are:

Principle 1: Instruction. RTI is first and foremost intended to prevent problems by optimizing language and literacy instruction. (In every chapter we have emphasized the importance of evidence-based instruction, and with English learners it is essential to ascertain whether the "evidence" included English learners in the study. Also, there is a body of evidence about what is effective specifically for teaching English learners.)

Principle 2: Responsive Teaching and Differentiation. The RTI process emphasizes increasingly differentiated and intensified instruction or intervention in language and literacy.

Principle 3: Assessment. An RTI approach demands assessment that can inform language and literacy instruction meaningfully. (As we have discussed, assessments for screening, progress monitoring, and diagnostic purposes must be culturally and linguistically appropriate.)

Principle 4: Collaboration. RTI requires a dynamic, positive, and productive collaboration among professionals with relevant expertise in language and literacy. Success also depends on strong and respectful partnerships among professionals, parents, and students. (We would add that relevant expertise includes second language acquisition and familiarity with students' cultures.)

Principle 5: Systemic and Comprehensive Approaches. RTI must be part of a comprehensive, systemic approach to language and literacy assessment and instruction that supports all preK–12 students and teachers (including ESL and bilingual specialists).

Principle 6: Expertise. All students have the right to receive instruction from well-prepared teachers who keep up-to-date and supplemental instruction from professionals specifically prepared to teach language and literacy. (Again, "well-prepared" includes knowledge about second language acquisition, effective pedagogical practices for English learners, implications of culture on learning, and, when possible, instructional support in the students' home language.)

Questions to Guide RTI with English Learners

The extent to which the following questions guide program development results in either successful RTI implementation or the creation of barriers to effective RTI implementation. As teams develop their RTI plan, make decisions about implementation, discuss resource allocation, and consider professional development priorities, they should ask themselves the following:

1. Have English learners had sufficient opportunity to learn (time and quality of instruction)?

2. Does Tier 1 instruction reflect best practice, and is it being implemented to a high degree?

3. Are our teachers respectful of and supportive of English learner students' cultures and language learning needs?

4. Are we committed to using only evidence-based intervention and curriculum?

5. How will we oversee fidelity of implementation?

6. Are we giving our English learners enough time in Tiers 2 and 3 before considering special education services?

7. Are teachers highly qualified in their content areas and also in effective teaching for English learners?

8. Are we utilizing the expertise on our staff in a collaborative way to provide a comprehensive instructional program for all students, including English learners (ESL, bilingual, general education teachers; specialists; administrators)?

9. Are we asking every member of the staff to contribute some time to RTI so that it is in fact a schoolwide initiative?

10. What are we willing to give up in order to free up time for RTI?

These kinds of questions are important for strategic planning and for moving forward with RTI.

Frequently Asked Questions

Although there are no single answers to these questions, or quick and easy solutions, there are some common approaches that schools use to deal with the logistical concerns of RTI. The following represent a sampling of the most common questions we are asked as we conduct professional development on the topic of RTI and English learners:

1. What is the right way to implement RTI for English learners?

There is no one particular approach to or definition of RTI; the literature on RTI covers several core features that constitute an RTI framework (see the components in Figure 1.1 in Chapter 1, and the principles of a successful RTI program and guiding questions for English learners in this chapter). RTI involves a significant change in the way schools have done business in the past, and if schools are going to make AYP targets and meet the needs of all students, then the way RTI will be implemented in a given district or building will depend on the issues discussed in this book and plan that is developed.

2. What is the role of special education teachers in RTI?

Teachers certified to work with students with mild to moderate disabilities, including learning disabilities, would continue to provide direct and indirect services to those students with IEPs. Ideally, however, the special education teacher would also have training in understanding the educational needs of English learners. With RTI, their expanded role would include providing consultation to teams (grade level, multidisciplinary or RTI teams) and sharing their expertise with colleagues as school personnel work together in a schoolwide effort.

3. **How do we get started with putting RTI in place? Do we begin with a whole building or the whole district?**

The decision of how to begin implementation of RTI depends largely on buy-in from stakeholders. If there is strong administrative support and the planning stage involved members from a variety of constituencies, then district-wide implementation may be effective. However, if there is a lot of resistance, consider starting small, with one grade level in elementary or one content area (reading or math) in secondary. It is important to implement RTI well and experience success. Once RTI is in place, the process serves as a model for getting others on board. Increased student achievement through effective RTI is the best "seller" of the program to others.

4. **Can RTI be used for determining special education eligibility?**

Yes. IDEA 2004 makes it clear that states are required to permit the use of RTI in determining special education eligibility (see Appendix A). However, the statute and its regulations don't specify RTI implementation (Zirkel & Krohn, 2008). RTI changes the nature of the comprehensive evaluation away from testing for eligibility and toward examining data that were collected on the student's instructional progress (including English language proficiency) for planning increasingly intense interventions. Some experts believe that testing for special education eligibility is unnecessary with RTI. Since districts can choose RTI or a discrepancy model, "there is no point in a discrepancy model if RTI is in place" (East, 2006).

5. **Who will conduct the intervention?**

Delivery of intervention varies widely and differs in Tier 2 and Tier 3 intervention. With a school-wide or grade-level model, scheduling is done at the administration level. Typically, school administrators determine what can be done given their personnel, resources, and master schedule. In most cases, the general education teacher conducts small group Tier 2 intervention during class time while other students are working independently. In other cases, intervention for students is provided during the time their class is elsewhere participating in programs such as P.E., art, music, foreign language, and computer lab. In secondary settings, a period of intervention may be part of a student's class schedule. (Keep in mind that intervention is designed to be temporary so that students receiving services do not miss out on these special programs or electives the entire year.) In other situations, someone other than the classroom teacher provides Tier 2 intervention. One creative district employs retired teachers to work with students before school and after school, other districts use existing personnel such as literacy coaches or reading specialists, and still others hold Saturday school taught by teachers or specialists.

For Tier 3 intervention, the increased intensity requires a greater level of expertise. The teacher or specialist providing Tier 3 intervention should be well-trained and have background in both literacy and teaching English learners effectively. So, it may be a special education teacher with knowledge of second language acquisition or a bilingual teacher or ESL specialist with expertise in literacy.

In terms of what research supports, the jury is still out. Most early reading studies with English learners that resembled Tier 2 interventions had interventions that were supplementary to general classroom instruction and were delivered in small groups by

instructors other than the general classroom teacher (McMaster, Kung, Han, & Cao, 2008). As the research base on intervention grows, we will know more about ways to conduct interventions most effectively. In the meantime, district planning teams should make decisions that fit best with their local conditions.

6. Why is collaboration with colleagues important, and how do we do it?

Collaboration in grade-level teams, subject-area teams, or cross-disciplinary teams, commonly called a Professional Learning Community (PLC), has benefits that are undisputed, yet many schools struggle with getting teachers to embrace the idea as a priority in their professional lives. Danielson (2007) discusses the importance of collaboration and working together with colleagues. "During conversations about practice, particularly when such conversations are organized around a common framework, teachers are able to learn from one another and to thereby enrich their own teaching. It is this joint learning that makes the conversations so rich—and so valued." In our research on professional development for improving practice with English learners (Echevarria, Short, & Vogt, 2008), we also found that this process of collaboration and discussion is critical both to enriching the professional lives of educators and to ensuring that the components used in a given setting (SIOP® components for instruction and RTI components) are applied with fidelity.

Lack of time is the most common barrier to collaboration, which prevents teachers from exchanging ideas, jointly planning lessons, evaluating individual student progress on a regular basis, and discussing appropriate adaptations, modifications, and interventions. This barrier is real and not easily remedied. Some teams meet before or after school, during lunch, or during common planning periods. Some schools dismiss students early one day a week for meetings, whereas others use funding sources to pay for substitutes, for example, one day per month. Each school or district needs to create ways to increase time for collaboration, which should be part of an overall professional development program since the activities of these groups provide feedback to teachers around common goals and components of their RTI program.

In their book on collaboration, Honigsfeld and Dove (2010) suggest that teachers use the acrostic ESCROW to guide their PLC meetings:

Establish and stick to set meeting times.

Start by discussing big ideas and set essential learning goals.

Concentrate on areas of special difficulty for English learners: scaffolding learning, adapting content, modifying assignments, increasing oral language opportunities, and differentiating tasks.

Review previous lessons based on student performance data.

Overcome the need to always be in control.

Work toward common understanding of English learners' needs.

Some collaborative groups actually observe one another's teaching or provide feedback on each other's videotaped lessons. However in-depth, some level of collaboration is recommended in order to enhance professional growth and improve instruction for English learners—and all students.

7. What do we do if more than 50% of our school population qualifies for Tier 2 and Tier 3 instruction?

There are some districts with high numbers of English learners in predominantly low-income, underperforming schools. The majority of students are performing below grade level for many of the reasons discussed in Chapter 2. However, even in these challenging schools, instructional programs should offer high-quality teaching that connects with what students know and is meaningful to them and that provides many opportunities to be exposed to interesting, relevant text and discussions using academic language. There are many schools committed to high-quality instruction that are model programs and "beat the odds." We highlight one such class in Appendix C.

If schools are using funds to support costly Tier 2 and Tier 3 services for more than the expected number of students, then those schools might consider investing the funds in effective professional development in Tier 1. Unusually high numbers of students in Tiers 2 and 3 raise a red flag that Tier 1 general education instruction needs to be seriously evaluated. As mentioned in other chapters, all students can and will learn under the right circumstances; the emphasis needs to be on meeting English learners' language and academic needs in the general education classroom. Administrative support and commitment to improved instruction is imperative.

8. How do RTI and SIOP® "dovetail"?

The SIOP® Model is a framework for making instruction comprehensible for English learners. Its emphasis on academic language development, differentiated instruction, and providing access to the core make it applicable in all tiers of the RTI process. The features of the SIOP® Model are integrated throughout the components of RTI. For example, if ELs are to learn the components of reading, reach grade-level standards in all content areas, and develop English proficiency, Tier 1 instruction should reflect the features of the SIOP Model consistently. Content and language objectives are posted to guide instruction and learning. Also, Tier 1 teachers give specific attention to vocabulary development, provide information in multiple ways (visual clues, physical gestures), present ideas verbally and in writing, create frequent opportunities for meaningful oral language practice including working with peers, make instructions and expectations extremely clear, e.g., through modeling a procedure or completing together part of a task, differentiate instruction based on language proficiency or academic skill level, and provide additional opportunities for practice. Many of these same features are necessary for making Tier 2 intervention effective for English learners. Even if Tier 2 intervention is a specific curriculum, teachers need to reflect on the SIOP features to make sure that they are providing optimal instruction at Tier 2, instruction that is understandable and that develops students' English language proficiency during intervention. At Tier 3, intervention is more intensive, and is provided in groups of 1–3 students. However, English learners still benefit from the features of the SIOP Model within the context of Tier 3 intervention. An English learner needs to understand the teacher's expectations and the language she uses, as well as have sufficient opportunity to practice skills and have a chance to use academic language in meaningful ways. So, the RTI process and the SIOP Model work together, hand in glove, to support the learning of English learners.

9. Does an ideal RTI model exist?

There are a number of states and districts that have implemented effective RTI approaches. A single ideal RTI model will probably never exist because research comparing different ways of reforming service delivery systems in schools is complex and may not be relevant as conditions vary from state to state and region to region. One of the reasons we included the Guide to Effective RTI in this book is so that readers can consider their own particular situation, take the information provided in each chapter and develop an RTI plan that suits the needs of your school's and district's student population.

For specific examples of RTI approaches, we direct readers to two excellent websites that feature RTI programs. One, from the National Center on Response to Intervention, includes an RTI state data base that provides a snapshot of each state's RTI implementation to date and is found at http://state.rti4success.org/. The other website is from the Pennsylvania Training and Technical Assistance Network, http://www.pattan.net/teachlead/ResponsetoIntervention.aspx, and provides many resources including an RTI Implementation Guide.

10. How does the ESL program work within an RTI process for English learners?

RTI is a comprehensive schoolwide service delivery model designed to offer evidence-based instruction to students and, based on assessment data, adjustments are made to increase academic success for all students. In the past, programs within schools, e.g., ESL, special education, Title 1, have operated as silos, separate from one another with little interaction or collaboration. Sometimes, in fact, school personnel feel threatened that a process like RTI may minimize their role or even eliminate their position. Quite the opposite is true. With RTI, the role of the ESL teacher could be expanded. He or she would continue to provide much-needed English language development services to students (even if they receive Tier 2 or Tier 3 literacy intervention) but might also serve as a team member on the problem-solving team. Their expertise makes a valuable contribution to discussions about struggling English learners. Bottom line: The idea of RTI is to provide the services students need so English learners would continue to receive specialized ESL instruction as needed.

Final Thoughts

In this chapter we have discussed some of the factors that contribute to successful RTI as well as some barriers to implementation. We also provided responses to frequently asked questions about RTI implementation. In large part, RTI is in its infancy, and as programs become more common, logistical concerns and other issues will be resolved—and new issues may arise. When considering the needs of English learners, it is important to keep their well-being at the forefront of decision-making and rely on what we currently know about effective instructional practices.

Sec. 300.307 Specific learning disabilities

(a) General. A State must adopt, consistent with Sec. 300.309, criteria for determining whether a child has a specific learning disability as defined in Sec. 300.8(c)(10). In addition, the criteria adopted by the State–

(1) Must not require the use of a severe discrepancy between intellectual ability and achievement for determining whether a child has a specific learning disability, as defined in Sec. 300.8(c)(10);

(2) Must permit the use of a process based on the child's response to scientific, research-based intervention; and

(3) May permit the use of other alternative research-based procedures for determining whether a child has a specific learning disability, as defined in Sec. 300.8(c)(10).

(b) Consistency with State criteria. A public agency must use the State criteria adopted pursuant to paragraph (a) of this section in determining whether a child has a specific learning disability.

(Authority: 20 U.S.C. 1221e-3; 1401(30); 1414(b)(6))

Sec. 300.309 Determining the existence of a specific learning disability

(a) The group described in Sec. 300.306 may determine that a child has a specific learning disability, as defined in Sec. 300.8(c)(10), if–

(1) The child does not achieve adequately for the child's age or to meet State-approved grade-level standards in one or more of the following areas, when provided with learning experiences and instruction appropriate for the child's age or State-approved grade-level standards:

(i) Oral expression.

(ii) Listening comprehension.

(iii) Written expression.

(iv) Basic reading skill.

(v) Reading fluency skills.

(vi) Reading comprehension.

(vii) Mathematics calculation.

(viii) Mathematics problem solving.

(2)

(i) The child does not make sufficient progress to meet age or State-approved grade-level standards in one or more of the areas identified in paragraph (a)(1) of this section when using a process based on the child's response to scientific, research-based intervention; or

(ii) The child exhibits a pattern of strengths and weaknesses in performance, achievement, or both, relative to age, State-approved grade-level standards, or intellectual development, that is determined by the group to be relevant to the identification of a specific learning disability, using appropriate assessments, consistent with Sec. Sec. 300.304 and 300.305; and

(3) The group determines that its findings under paragraphs (a)(1) and (2) of this section are not primarily the result of–

(i)   A visual, hearing, or motor disability;

(ii)   Mental retardation;

(iii) Emotional disturbance;

(iv) Cultural factors;

(v)   Environmental or economic disadvantage; or

(vi) Limited English proficiency.

(b) To ensure that underachievement in a child suspected of having a specific learning disability is not due to lack of appropriate instruction in reading or math, the group must consider, as part of the evaluation described in Sec. Sec. 300.304 through 300.306–

(1) Data that demonstrate that prior to, or as a part of, the referral process, the child was provided appropriate instruction in regular education settings, delivered by qualified personnel; and

(2) Data-based documentation of repeated assessments of achievement at reasonable intervals, reflecting formal assessment of student progress during instruction, which was provided to the child's parents.

(c) The public agency must promptly request parental consent to evaluate the child to determine if the child needs special education and related services, and must adhere to the timeframes described in Sec. Sec. 300.301 and 300.303, unless extended by mutual written agreement of the child's parents and a group of qualified professionals, as described in Sec. 300.306(a)(1)–

(1) If, prior to a referral, a child has not made adequate progress after an appropriate period of time when provided instruction, as described in paragraphs (b)(1) and (b)(2) of this section; and

(2) Whenever a child is referred for an evaluation.

(Authority: 20 U.S.C. 1221e-3; 1401(30); 1414(b)(6))

Source:

http://idea.ed.gov/explore/view/p/%2Croot%2Cregs%2C300%2CD%2C300%252E307%2C

appendix b: SIOP protocol

The Sheltered Instruction Observation Protocol (SIOP®)
(Echevarria, Vogt, & Short, 2000; 2004; 2008)

Observer(s): _____   Teacher: _____
Date: _____   School: _____
Grade: _____   Class/Topic: _____
ESL Level: _____   Lesson: Multi-day Single-day *(circle one)*

Total Points Possible: 120 (Subtract 4 points for each NA given) _____
Total Points Earned: _____   Percentage Score: _____

Directions: Circle the number that best reflects what you observe in a sheltered lesson. You may give a score from 0–4 (or NA on selected items). Cite under "Comments" specific examples of the behaviors observed.

	Highly Evident		Somewhat Evident		Not Evident	
Preparation	**4**	**3**	**2**	**1**	**0**	
1. **Content objectives** clearly defined, displayed, and reviewed with students	❑	❑	❑	❑	❑	
2. **Language objectives** clearly defined, displayed, and reviewed with students	❑	❑	❑	❑	❑	
3. **Content concepts** appropriate for age and educational background level of students	❑	❑	❑	❑	❑	
4. **Supplementary materials** used to a high degree, making the lesson clear and meaningful (e.g., computer programs, graphs, models, visuals)	❑	❑	❑	❑	❑	
5. **Adaptation of content** (e.g., text, assignment) to all levels of student proficiency	❑	❑	❑	❑	❑	
6. **Meaningful activities** that integrate lesson concepts (e.g., surveys, letter writing, simulations, constructing models) with language practice opportunities for reading, writing, listening, and/or speaking	❑	❑	❑	❑	❑	

Comments:

	4	**3**	**2**	**1**	**0**	**NA**
Building Background						
7. **Concepts explicitly linked** to students' background experiences	❑	❑	❑	❑	❑	❑
8. **Links explicitly made** between past learning and new concepts	❑	❑	❑	❑	❑	
9. **Key vocabulary** emphasized (e.g., introduced, written, repeated, and highlighted for students to see)	❑	❑	❑	❑	❑	

Comments:

	4	**3**	**2**	**1**	**0**	
Comprehensible Input						
10. **Speech** appropriate for students' proficiency level (e.g., slower rate, enunciation, and simple sentence structure for beginners)	❑	❑	❑	❑	❑	
11. **Clear explanation** of academic tasks	❑	❑	❑	❑	❑	
12. **A variety of techniques** used to make content concepts clear (e.g., modeling, visuals, hands-on activities, demonstrations, gestures, body language)	❑	❑	❑	❑	❑	

Comments:

	4	**3**	**2**	**1**	**0**	
Strategies						
13. Ample opportunities provided for students to use **learning strategies**	❑	❑	❑	❑	❑	

	Highly Evident		Somewhat Evident		Not Evident	
	4	3	2	1	0	
14. **Scaffolding techniques** consistently used assisting and supporting student understanding (e.g., think-alouds)	❑	❑	❑	❑	❑	
15. **A variety of questions or tasks that promote higher-order thinking skills** (e.g., literal, analytical, and interpretive questions) *Comments:*	❑	❑	❑	❑	❑	

Interaction	4	3	2	1	0	
16. Frequent opportunities for **interaction** and discussion between teacher/student and among students, which encourage elaborated responses about lesson concepts	❑	❑	❑	❑	❑	
17. **Grouping configurations** support language and content objectives of the lesson	❑	❑	❑	❑	❑	
18. Sufficient **wait time for student responses** consistently provided	❑	❑	❑	❑	❑	NA
19. Ample opportunities for students to **clarify key concepts in L1** as needed with aide, peer, or L1 text *Comments:*	❑	❑	❑	❑	❑	❑

Practice/Application	4	3	2	1	0	NA
20. **Hands-on materials and/or manipulatives** provided for students to practice using new content knowledge	❑	❑	❑	❑	❑	❑
21. Activities provided for students to **apply content and language knowledge** in the classroom	❑	❑	❑	❑	❑	NA ❑
22. Activities integrate all **language skills** (i.e., reading, writing, listening, and speaking) *Comments:*	❑	❑	❑	❑	❑	

Lesson Delivery	4	3	2	1	0	
23. **Content objectives** clearly supported by lesson delivery	❑	❑	❑	❑	❑	
24. **Language objectives** clearly supported by lesson delivery	❑	❑	❑	❑	❑	
25. **Students engaged** approximately 90% to 100% of the period	❑	❑	❑	❑	❑	
26. **Pacing** of the lesson appropriate to students' ability level *Comments:*	❑	❑	❑	❑	❑	

Review/Assessment	4	3	2	1	0	
27. Comprehensive **review of key vocabulary**	❑	❑	❑	❑	❑	
28. Comprehensive **review of key content concepts**	❑	❑	❑	❑	❑	
29. Regular **feedback** provided to students on their output (e.g., language, content, work)	❑	❑	❑	❑	❑	
30. **Assessment of student comprehension and learning** of all lesson objectives (e.g., spot checking, group response) throughout the lesson *Comments:*	❑	❑	❑	❑	❑	

appendix c: using students' backgrounds for academic success

**by Vicki Roberts, Professional Development Specialist-Title I; Intermediate ELA
and Lina Nino, Grade 4 Teacher**

**Shorehaven Elementary School, Garland Independent School District
Dr. Patricia Tremmel, Principal**

I began by taking a list of stories, which I called my "Treasure Chest" (see Figure A.1). I told the students that all of the stories about your life are treasures you hold in your chest. Then I chose a story about my fifth birthday from my Treasure Chest (see Figure A.1). Next, I showed them a storyboard I had created to show the story I wanted to tell (see Figure A.3). I used the storyboard to talk out my story with the class. Once that was done, I showed them my written story (see Figure A.4). I also showed them a story written from the storyboard that wasn't as interesting and we talked about the differences between the elaborated one and the "boring" story (see Figure A.2).

Once this activity was done, I read off the rest of the items on my Treasure Chest (see Figure A.1), and I had the students create their own Treasure Chests. Ms. Nino made one as well. When they had finished, all students read their lists from their Treasure Chests aloud. This process generated more topics as students' memories were jogged when they heard about events similar to ones they had also experienced. Those topics were added to their lists. When we were done, all the students had a long list on their Treasure Chests.

Next, students chose a story from their Treasure Chest that they wanted to write about. Using my storyboard as an example, they created their own storyboards. As they began a quick sketch of the story they wanted to tell, I told them to close their eyes and visualize their story as if it were happening right now. I always have them write in active voice, which tends to bring out their "voice" and much more elaboration. I encourage them to tell the story moment-by-moment. I tell them that they are the stars of their life stories.

Once their storyboards were complete, students had to tell a partner their story using the storyboard. Their partners were free to ask any unanswered questions that the storyteller might have forgotten to mention or that the listener was curious about. Doing this helps writers come up with even more ideas and details for their stories.

Next, the students began writing their stories in the same way they told their stories. To assist their writing, I provided the children with their own personal dictionary to use during the year. Although this dictionary contained many frequently used words, homophones, etc., it also had blanks for students to write in their own frequently used words. Writers have a tendency to use many of the same words over and over in their writing. By having their own frequently used words written correctly in their personal dictionary, they more readily take ownership of the words they use.

While they wrote, Ms. Nino and I walked around and talked with individual students, helping them through the process. In order to discourage their thought processes from being interrupted, they were told to spell difficult words the best they could, but to circle them, and Ms. Nino or I would help them with the spelling later. Relieved of having to be

FIGURE A.1 *My Treasure Chest*

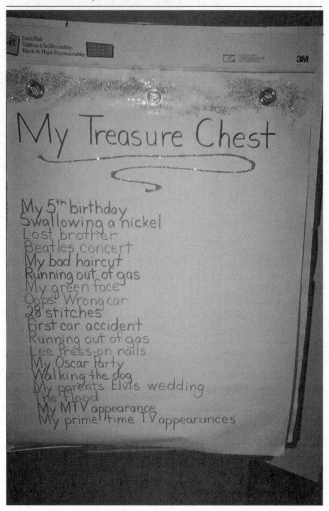

perfect, the students wrote without anxiety, and they were writing about their own real life experiences!

Once they finished writing their stories, the next step was to read them aloud to the class. I never told whose story I was reading, but I told them if they wanted everyone to know that they were the writer, then they could raise their hand and I would make the announcement. We talked about all the things we loved about the story. If there was something I particularly liked, I would stop and reread the part again, OOOHing and AAAHing over it. (The students immediately began using that "AAH" example in their next piece of writing.)

As the stories were read aloud, Ms. Nino and I kept a sticky note handy to jot down mini-lessons the class could work on based on the problems they were having with their papers. We taught a mini-lesson by modeling the skill; then students practiced it to ensure mastery. We encouraged the students to use the new (or refined) skill in their next piece of writing.

The emphasis of our approach was to show them, not tell them, even with the mini-lessons. We did a great deal of taking parts of their writing and showing them how

FIGURE A.2 *Boring* **My Fifth Birthday** *Story*

It was my birthday. My friends said happy birthday to me. We had cake. It was good. There was a Merry-go-round in the front yard. We rode it. It was fun. I opened presents. I gave my friends candy. It was a great birthday.

to inject emotion into the piece with dialogue. We brainstormed things you would say when you're excited, scared, worried, and so forth. As a result, we noticed how they started to incorporate dialogue and emotion into their writing. Again, modeling was key.

We never assessed papers in private. If a child writes a paper and the teacher marks it up and hands it back, what has he learned? The teacher has learned that she can't teach writing, and the student learns that he can't write. My advice: Share their writing! If writers never hear a good piece of writing, they will never be able to create a good piece of writing. You will always get what you've always got. Sharing writing is valuable for everyone! The students begin emulating what they hear. They begin to become great writers.

Ms. Nino also had a treasure chest of stories from which to write. She always modeled her own piece before assigning a new piece of writing to her students. I think it is important for the teacher to write whatever she requires her students to write. Students need to see the thinking, the scribbled out revisions, the hesitations, and the mistakes. Students need to see writing as a process. The finished product is really never written perfectly the first time. All writers go through a process of creation, frustration, and ultimately elation when the piece is complete. Each time a new assignment was given, students had a choice to start on a new piece, or to use an old piece and "kick it up a notch!"

By modeling, talking, writing, and sharing, the results were astounding! However, I felt the most powerful factors were the modeling and the fact that the students wrote about their **own** experiences. Not writing from contrived writing prompts and writing

FIGURE A.3 *Storyboard*

FIGURE A.4 *Elaborated* **My Fifth Birthday Story**

It was my birthday!

"Happy birthday!" shouted my friends. I couldn't believe it. I was finally five years old. I could go to kindergarten! I was grown up! It was the day I had been waiting for, and it was finally here.

We had cake.

In walked my mother with a chocolate birthday cake. It was the prettiest cake I'd ever seen. It was iced with white icing and big pink roses. I couldn't wait to bite into it! I could just taste the big pink rose melting in my mouth.

There was a Merry-Go-Round in the front yard.

"Look out the window," said my dad. When I looked out the window, I couldn't believe my eyes! There in my own front yard was a merry-go-round! It was red and white striped just like a candy cane with four beautiful horses. Pinch me, I must be dreaming!

We rode it. It was fun.

"Let's go ride the horses!" I screamed. We ran out the door as fast as we could. My favorite color is purple, so I jumped up on the purple carousel horse. It was beautiful with a gold saddle and ruby eyes. I felt like a queen on top of this magical horse. We all looked like royalty riding the magical horses. We rode round and round until we felt dizzy with excitement.

Then we opened the presents.

"Time to open presents," announced my mom. "Open mine first!" all of my friends shouted. I tore into the specially wrapped gifts. I received all my favorite things: four different colors of Play-Doh, a Barbie, the one with the black striped bathing suit and black ponytail, and a paint by number oil painting set. Was I a lucky girl!

Then I gave my friends a goody bag.

Now it was time for me to give my friends their goody bags. I gave them each a sack filled with all my favorite candy: miniature Hershey bars, Bazooka bubblegum, and Tootsie Roll pops. It had been an exciting day. Although this birthday happened forty-six years ago, it's one birthday I always remember.

about their own life experiences enabled them to be the expert in their experience. This created expert writers! 16/17 students passed, but 11/17 were commended! You must attain a score of 3 or 4 on the composition, 4 being the highest score, to achieve commended status! One of Ms. Nino's students even achieved a perfect score, meaning 100% on the objective part of the test (editing and revision) and a 4 on the composition! It still brings tears to my eyes!

As an example of the writing progress students in Ms. Nino's class experienced, see the difference between student Juan Garcia's writing in November and a few months later in February. As you can see, he still needs instruction in refining his writing skills such as use of conventions but the growth in this English learner's written expression is impressive.

My favret Place to go is Mexico.
Becuse there are many tipe of animals
like if it was the zoo exept the animals
are free. They get to be up to the Bigest
mountian. They even get randover some
times they starb to death or slip and die ar leavi
The reson I like Mexico is becuse I was
born in Mexico. I like Mexico becuse
they do a lot of Partys wedin even
Rodeo's fiften's they even celebra
March 19. The People Pop fireworks.
The People Pop the Bigest fireworks made
in Mexico. ON March 12 they celebrate
god and son god with fireworks too.

I got up at 11:00 O'clock.
I put on my luky shirt, pants
and boots. I put my cowboy hat
on. I ran down stairs. Eggs I
hate eggs but oh well I'm
hungry finished now I just need
To wait for my pearents done
they said. On the way there
I saw cows, bulls, horses and
donkies hey dad. I can see
the rodeo. Finally we got
there. I thought I was
going to be sick thud ouch
my leg fel asleep. I'm going
to the back I saw the bull
I was going to ride. It was
big and scary but I was
not afraid I was trying
to be tough I saw the
anawncer and told him to
let me ride that bull
okey he replied but get
redy to come out. ladies
and Jentel men he yelled
the most smallest bull
rider from san Jose de cerbANtes

Juan Garcia thank you.
They took us to the back
I sat on the bull the door
opened aaah the bull din't
give up on the Jumping. I
couldn't hold no longer
until I dug my heel in the
bulls meat bush ouch I
started running becuse the
bull was going after me.
bush ouch the bulls horns
hurt. Time to anounce the
winers 3rd Place Javier my
cusen 2nd Jose my brother Mar
I'm not going to win 1st Place
Juan Garcia yeah thats
my boy my mom and DaD
yealled thank you I was
so glad that I started
to crie DaD afer here
could go to Golden coral.
That was the most funyest
thing that hapend to me
in my life.

Select one of the following case studies for an English learner in elementary, middle, or high school. Based on the profile presented, be prepared to discuss the following questions with a group of educators.

Case Study #1: Marisela (third grade)

Marisela is a nine-year-old girl who attends ABC Elementary School. She is a high-risk student who was born prematurely and was in the hospital for three months due to low birth weight. She attended a parochial school kindergarten and repeated kindergarten in public school. A native-Spanish speaker, at the end of kindergarten Marisela did not recognize any of the letters of the English alphabet and was only able to identify her name in print. She had difficulty retaining information and needed a great deal of teacher redirection to complete tasks. She ended first grade as a non-reader who, while able to recognize consonant sounds, did not recognize vowels, and could not segment or blend CVC words. Marisela had a bank of ten high-frequency words, and was beginning to establish one-to-one word pointing and to focus on the print in text. Marisela became very frustrated when any new concept was introduced and refused to participate or try to do her work without one-on-one teacher help or extra support from the bilingual aide.

Based on the information provided above, discuss the following questions:

- What might be some possible causes for a mismatch between Marisela's personal and educational background and the content she is being taught?
- What questions would you want to ask Marisela's teacher about the instructional approaches that are being used in the classroom?
- What information should you seek before determining that the current classroom instruction is inappropriate for Marisela's needs? Re-examine the figure "Classroom Accommodations/Modifications for English Learners" on page 45 in this book. Which, if any, of the recommendations might be appropriate for Marisela? How could the teacher monitor Marisela's progress on the accommodations you have selected?
- Many teachers have difficulty using reading assessment findings to tailor instruction for groups of students who are struggling. As a peer coach or administrator for Marisela's teacher, what advice, assistance, or recommendations might you provide in order to help the teacher better utilize the information he or she already has about Marisela?
- Revisit the SIOP® Model features in the SIOP® protocol found in Appendix B. Based on Marisela's profile, which of the features are especially important if she is to be successful in the classroom setting?

Case Study #2: Jacinto (sixth grade)

Jacinto is an eleven-year-old boy who has lived and attended school in the United States for the past three years. He has been receiving intensive ESL instruction and support for one hour each day during each school year. Jacinto's older brother, Gaspar, who is fourteen

and in ninth grade, has adjusted well to his teachers and classes, and seems to be thriving both academically and in learning English. Gaspar attended ESL classes during sixth and seventh grades. The boys' parents, although not fluent in English, are very concerned about and involved in their sons' schooling. They do what they can to help with homework assignments and make it clear that the boys are to be respectful to their teachers and do what they say.

Jacinto, unlike his older brother, has struggled academically since his family arrived from Guatemala when he was nine. His teachers have reported distractibility, an unwillingness to participate in class activities, a reluctance to learn and practice English, and serious academic gaps in reading and math. In fifth grade, Jacinto nearly failed several subjects. However, his teacher, feeling that the boy's English language proficiency was limited, gave Jacinto a D on his report card for both science and social studies, and a C− in math because he seemed to try hard during the math period.

Now that Jacinto is in sixth grade, the reading and content demands have substantially increased, and Jacinto is again performing poorly. He seldom completes homework assignments, frequently telling his parents that his teachers don't assign it. He is no longer receiving intensive English instruction with the ESL teacher, and he's beginning to talk with his friends about dropping out of school as soon as he reaches his sixteenth birthday.

Based on the information provided about Jacinto, discuss the following questions:

- What might be some possible causes for a mismatch between Jacinto's personal and educational background and the content he is being taught?
- What questions would you want to ask Jacinto's teachers about the instructional approaches that are being used in the classroom?
- What information should you seek before determining that the current classroom instruction is inappropriate for Jacinto's needs?
- Re-examine the figure "Classroom Accommodations/Modifications" on page 45 of this book. Which, if any, of the recommendations might be appropriate for Jacinto? How could the teacher monitor Jacinto's progress on the accommodations/ modifications you have selected?
- Many teachers have difficulty using reading assessment findings to tailor instruction for groups of students who are struggling. As a peer coach or administrator for Jacinto's teacher, what advice, assistance, or recommendations might you provide in order to help the teacher better utilize the information he or she already has about Jacinto?
- Revisit the SIOP® Model features in the SIOP® protocol found in Appendix B. Based on Jacinto's profile, which of the features are especially important if he is to be successful in the classroom setting?

Case Study #3: Tran (tenth grade)

Tran is a second-generation Vietnamese American who was born in southern California. While Vietnamese is his first language, Tran is fluent conversationally in English. A gregarious boy with an infectious smile, he is well liked by his peers and teachers alike. Because he has attended his local neighborhood schools since kindergarten, Tran

is comfortable navigating through high school and he is somewhat a "big man on campus," primarily because of his leadership skills and engaging personality.

Academically, Tran is having difficulties in his tenth grade classes, especially in those that require a great deal of reading. For many years, he has been able to "coast," periodically succumbing to "fake reading," whereby he pretends to read assignments both in class and at home, but in reality he's simply picking out words he recognizes. He frequently talks to his friends about their assignments and to this point he has been able to glean key information and concepts where he can, in order to maintain a C average. But, this year Tran's inability to read comprehensively has caught up with him and he's in danger of failing. Several of his teachers have expressed concern about how Tran is performing, yet Tran dismisses their concerns, telling them that he'll start studying harder to improve his grades.

Based on the information provided about Tran, discuss the following questions:

- What might be some possible causes for a mismatch between Tran's personal and educational background and the content he is being taught?
- What questions would you want to ask Tran's teachers about the instructional approaches that are being used in the classroom?
- What information should you seek before determining that the current classroom instruction is inappropriate for Tran's needs?
- Re-examine the figure "Classroom Accommodations/Modifications" on p. 45 of this book. Which, if any, of the recommendations might be appropriate for Tran? How could the teacher monitor Tran's progress on the accommodations/modifications you have selected?
- Many teachers have difficulty using reading assessment findings to tailor instruction for groups of students who are struggling. As a peer coach or administrator for Tran's teacher, what advice, assistance, or recommendations might you provide in order to help the teacher better utilize the information he or she already has about Tran?
- Revisit the SIOP® Model features in the SIOP® protocol found in Appendix B. Based on Tran's profile, which of the features are especially important if he is to be successful in the classroom setting?

Academic language: Language proficiency associated with schooling, and the abstract language abilities required for academic work; a more complex, conceptual, linguistic ability that includes analysis, synthesis, and evaluation. Academic language and vocabulary can be generic across content areas, or unique for each type of content, and both represent considerable challenges for English learners and struggling readers.

Additive bilingualism: Rather than neglecting or rejecting students' home language and culture, additive bilingualism promotes building on what home language knowledge the child brings to the classroom and adding to it.

Adequate Yearly Progress (AYP): Integral to the No Child Left Behind (NCLB) legislation, this term refers to the annual minimum growth needed to meet the requirements of NCLB within a specified timeframe.

Assessment: The orderly process of gathering, analyzing, interpreting, and reporting student performance, ideally from multiples sources over a period of time; also, the broad process of obtaining information used in decision-making about a student, group of students, curriculum, program, or educational policy.

Baseline data: Basic information on a student's current performance level, which is gathered before a program or intervention begins. It is the starting point to be used to compare a student's learning before a program of instruction begins.

Benchmarks: Content or developmental standards that describe sequences of growth that allow progress monitoring over time.

Benchmark assessment: The periodic assessment (a minimum of three times a year) of all students compared to age or grade-level standards.

Bilingual instruction: School instruction using two languages, generally the native language of a student and a second language. The amount of time that each language is used depends on the type of bilingual program, its specific objectives, and students' levels of language proficiency.

Collaborative team: A group of people at a school or district who meet on a scheduled or as-need basis to fulfill a specific purpose or function. Collaborative teams in RTI may include teachers, parents, administrators, and other interested community members who work in co-operation, with shared goals, and perceived outcomes occurring in a climate of trust.

Communicative competence: The combination of grammatical, discourse, strategic, and sociolinguistic competence that allows the recognition and production of fluent and appropriate language in all communication settings.

Content-based ESL: An instructional approach in which content topics are used as the vehicle for second language learning. A system of instruction in which teachers use a variety of instructional techniques as a way of developing second language, content, cognitive, and study skills.

Content standards: Definitions of what students are expected to know and be capable of doing for a given content area; the knowledge and skills that need to be taught in order for students to reach competency; what students are expected to learn and what schools are expected to teach. There may be national, state, or local-level standards.

Core curriculum: The planned instruction in a content area, which is central and usually mandatory for all students of a school (e.g., reading, math, science).

Curriculum-Based Measurements (CBM): A concise method used to find out how students are progressing in basic academic areas such as math, reading, writing, and spelling; CBM are widely available and well-researched tools for collecting ongoing assessment data during intervention.

Data-based decision-making: The use of student assessment data to guide the design, implementation, and adjustment of instruction; considered by some to be synonymous with progress monitoring because both require the collection and use of data.

Differentiated instruction: Instruction that matches the specific strengths and needs of each learner; includes providing alterations to curriculum, instruction, and assessment that recognize students' varying background knowledge, language proficiency, and academic abilities.

Early intervention services: A set of coordinated services for students in kindergarten through grade 12 (with particular emphasis on students in kindergarten through grade 3) who are not currently identified as needing special education or related services, but who need additional academic and behavioral support to succeed in general education.

Engagement: When students are fully taking part in a lesson, they are said to be engaged. This is a holistic term that encompasses listening, reading, writing, responding, and discussing. The level of students' engagement during a lesson may be assessed to a greater or lesser degree.

English learners (ELs): Children and adults who are learning English as a second or additional language. This

term may apply to learners across various levels of proficiency in English. ELs may also be referred to as English language learners (ELLs), non-English speaking (NES), limited-English speaking (LES), and a non-native speaker (NNS).

ESL: English as a second language; used to refer to programs and classes to teach students English as a second (or additional) language.

Evaluation: Judgments about students' learning made by interpreting and analyzing assessment data; the process of judging achievement, growth, product, processes, or changes in these; judgments of education programs. The process of assessment and evaluation can be viewed as progressive: first, assessment; then, evaluation.

Explicit instruction: Instruction that is clear, deliberate, and visible.

Fidelity: Instructional programs, methods, or models are implemented with intensity, accuracy, and consistency; using a program or method of instruction as it was intended to be used.

Five "Big Ideas" or pillars of Reading: Critical aspects of reading for all RTI tiers: phonemic awareness, phonics, fluency, vocabulary, and comprehension; many reading experts believe the "big ideas" represent a narrow view of the process of reading. Allington (2008) recommends an additional five "big ideas" that are particularly relevant to RTI: (1) classroom organization; (2) matching pupils to texts; (3) access to interesting texts, choice, and collaboration; (4) writing and reading as natural, reciprocal processes; and (5) expert tutoring.

Grouping: The assignment of students into groups of classes for instruction, such as by age, ability, or achievement; or within classes, such as by reading ability, proficiency, language background, or interests. **Flexible grouping** enables students to move among different groups based on their performance and instructional strengths and needs.

Home language: The language or languages spoken in the student's home by people who live there; also referred to as first language (L1), primary language, mother tongue, or native language.

Instructional intervention: Clear, deliberate, and carefully planned instruction delivered by trained personnel tailored to meet the identified needs of struggling students.

Intensive intervention: Explicit and systematic instruction delivered by highly skilled teacher specialists that provides students with increased opportunities for guided practice and teacher feedback. This instruction is targeted and tailored to meet the needs of struggling learners in small groups.

Measurement: Refers to the procedure of assigning scores or numbers to describe the degree to which a student has acquired a particular skill or attribute.

Native English speaker: An individual whose first language is English. Native language is an individual's first, primary, or home language (L1).

No Child Left Behind Act of 2001 (NCLB): Also known as the reauthorization of the Elementary and Secondary Education Act (ESEA); under this legislation, all children must reach proficiency, as defined by each state's proficiency measures; requires annual testing in grades 3–8 and 11 in reading and mathematics; also requires disaggregated reporting of scores on an annual basis to the federal government.

Outcome assessment: The measurement of how students perform academically at the end of planned instruction or at the end of the year.

Scaffolding: Adult (e.g., teacher) support for learning and student performance of tasks through instruction, modeling, questioning, feedback, graphic organizers, and more, across successive lessons. These supports are gradually withdrawn ("gradual release of responsibility"), thus transferring more and more autonomy to the child. Scaffolding activities provide support for learning that should be removed as learners are able to demonstrate strategic behaviors in their own learning.

Scientifically based interventions: Scientifically based means research that involves the application of rigorous, systematic, and objective procedures to obtain reliable and valid knowledge relevant to educational activities and programs. Also referred to as evidence based interventions.

Sheltered instruction (SI): A means for making content comprehensible for English learners while they are developing English proficiency. Sheltered classrooms, which include a mix of native English speakers and English learners or only English learners, integrate language and content while infusing sociocultural awareness. **SDAIE**, Specially Designed Academic Instruction in English, is a term for sheltered instruction that is used in several states. It features strategies and techniques for making content understandable for English learners. Although some SDAIE techniques are research-based, SDAIE itself has not been scientifically validated.

SIOP® (Sheltered Instruction Observation Protocol): A scientifically validated model of sheltered instruction designed to make grade-level academic content understandable for English learners while at the same time developing their English language. The Protocol and lesson planning guide ensure that teachers are consistently implementing practices known to be effective for English learners.

Stages of language proficiency: Depending on where you live and teach, the labels for the following stages may be somewhat different, and there may be fewer or more designations. What follows are the stages of language

proficiency for English learners as listed in Vogt & Echevarria (2008, pp. 51–52). Remember that students at lower levels of English proficiency are not necessarily functioning at lower levels of cognitive ability. Frequently, these students are able to use higher level thinking skills in their primary language but have a more difficult time understanding academic content and expressing their knowledge in English.

1. *Beginning (Pre-Production):* English learners in this stage have little comprehension of oral and written English, and are unable to produce much, if any, English.

2. *Beginning (Early Production):* In this stage English learners have limited English comprehension but can now give one or two word oral responses.

3. *Intermediate (Early):* Students at this stage have some proficiency in communicating simple ideas and can comprehend contextualized information.

4. *Intermediate:* At this stage, English learners have proficiency in communicating ideas and comprehending contextualized information in English.

5. *Early Advanced:* These English learners can communicate well, have good comprehension of information, and have adequate vocabulary to achieve academically.

6. *Advanced:* Students at this stage have near native speech fluency, very good comprehension of information in English, and expanded vocabulary to achieve academically.

Subtractive bilingualism: The learning of a new language at the expense of the primary language. Learners often lose their native language and culture because they don't have opportunities to continue learning or using it, or they perceive that language to be of lower status. Loss of the primary language often leads to cultural ambivalence.

Supplemental intervention: Additional Tier 1 instruction targeted to meet specific language and literacy needs of individual students. Supplemental materials may be used that are aligned with and support the core instructional program.

Standard protocol: Intensive, short-term instructional interventions conducted with a small group of targeted students that follow a specified script and have research to support their effectiveness. The materials used supplement the general education curriculum.

Universal screening (school-wide screening): A quick-check assessment of all students' current level of performance in a content or skill area. This is administered three times per year.

Note: The terms and definitions in this Glossary have been adapted from the following sources: Echevarria, Vogt, & Short, 2008, pp. 244–247; *RTI for English Learners Institute Participant Workbook* (developed for Pearson by J. Echevarria & M.E. Vogt), 2009, pp. 77–79; and Pennsylvania Department of Education: *Response to Intervention. Framework for Secondary Schools: Guidelines and Recommendations*, 2008, pp. 23–26.

references

Adger, C., & Locke, J. (2000). *Broadening the base: School/community partnerships serving language minority students at risk.* Santa Cruz, CA: Center for Research on Education, Diversity & Excellence.

Ajayi, L. (2009). English as a second language learners' exploration of multimodal texts in a junior high school. *Journal of Adolescent & Adult Literacy, 52*(7), 585–595.

Allington, R. L. (2008). *What really matters in Response to Intervention: Research-based designs.* Boston, MA: Allyn & Bacon.

Allington, R. L., & Johnston, P. H. (2002). *Reading to learn: Lessons from exemplary fourth-grade classrooms.* New York, NY: Guilford.

Artiles, A. J., Kozleski, E., Trent, S., Osher, D., & Ortiz, A. (2010). Justifying and explaining disproportionality, 1968–2008: A critique of underlying views of culture. *Exceptional Children, 76,* 279–299.

Artiles, A. J., & Trent, S. (1994). Overrepresentation of minority students in special education: A continuing debate. *Journal of Special Education, 27,* 410–437.

August, D., Beck, I. L., Calderón, M., Francis, D. J., Lesaux, N. K., & Shanahan, T. (2008). Instruction and professional development. In D. August & T. Shanahan (Eds.), *Developing reading and writing in second-language learners* (pp. 131–250). New York, NY: Routledge; Washington, DC: Center for Applied Linguistics; Newark, DE: International Reading Association.

August, D., Carlo, M., Dressler, C., & Snow, C. (2005). The critical role of vocabulary development for English language learners. *Learning Disabilities Research and Practice, 20,* 50–57.

August, D., & Shanahan, T. (Eds.). (2006). *Developing literacy in second-language learners: A report of the National Literacy Panel on Language-Minority Children and Youth.* Mahwah, NJ: Lawrence Erlbaum Associates.

August, D., & Shanahan, T. (Eds.). (2008). *Developing reading and writing in second-language learners: Lessons from the Report of the National Literacy Panel on Language-Minority Children and Youth.* New York, NY: Routledge, the Center for Applied Linguistics, and the International Reading Association.

Baca, L., & Cervantes, H. (1984). *The bilingual special education interface.* St. Louis, MO: Times Mirror/Mosby.

Ballantyne, K. G., Sanderman, A. R., & Levy, J. (2008). *Educating English language learners: Building teacher capacity.* Washington, DC: National Clearinghouse for English Language Acquisition. Available at http://www.ncela.gwu.edu/practice/mainstream_teachers.htm

Barton, P., & Coley, R. (2009). Those persistent gaps. *Educational Leadership 67*(4), 18–23.

Batalova, J., Fix, M., & Murray, J. (2005). *English language learner adolescents: Demographics and literacy achievements.* Report to the Center for Applied Linguistics. Washington, DC: Migration Policy Institute.

Batsche, G., Elliott, J., Graden, J., Grimes, J., Kovaleski, J., Parsse, D., Reschly, D., Schrag, J., & Tilly, W. D. (2008). *Response to intervention: Policy considerations and implementation.* Alexandria, VA: National Association of State Directors of Special Education.

Bauer, E. B. (2009). Informed additive literacy instruction for ELLs. *The Reading Teacher, 62*(5), 446–448.

Bear, D., Helman, L., Templeton, S., Invernizzi, M., & Johnston, F. (2007). *Words their way for English learners: Word study for phonics, vocabulary, and spelling instruction.* Upper Saddle River, NJ: Pearson/Merrill Prentice Hall.

Beck, L., McKeown, M., & Kucan, L. (2002). *Bringing words to life: Robust vocabulary instruction.* New York, NY: Guilford.

Biancarosa, G., & Snow, C. (2004). *Reading next: A vision for action and research in middle and high school literacy.* Report to the Carnegie Corporation of New York. Washington, DC: Alliance for Excellent Education.

Blachowicz, C. L. Z., Fisher, P., Ogle, D., & Watts-Taffe, S. (2006). Vocabulary: Questions from the classroom. *Reading Research Quarterly, 41,* 524–539.

Black, R. W. (2009). English-language learners, fan communities, and 21st-century skills. *Journal of Adolescent and Adult Literacy, 52*(8), 688–697.

Bottoms, G. (2007). Treat all students like the "best" students. *Educational Leadership, 64*(7), 30–37.

Brophy, J., & Good, T. (1970). Teacher's communication of differential expectations for children's classroom performance: Some behavioral data. *Journal of Educational Psychology, 61,* 365–374.

Brozo, W. G. (2010). Response to Intervention or responsive instruction? Challenges and possibilities of Response to Intervention for adolescent literacy. *Journal of Adolescent & Adult Literacy, 53*(4), 277–281.

Capps, R., Fix, M., Murray, J., Ost, J., Passel, J., & Herwantoro, S. (2005). *The new demography of America's schools: Immigration and the No Child Left Behind Act.* Washington, DC: The Urban Institute.

Cardenes-Hagan, E. (2007). *English language learners with learning disabilities.* Webcast retrieved on January 25,

2010 from www.colorincolorado.org/powerpoint/ webcast2007.ppt.

Carlo, M. S., August, D., McLaughlin, B., Snow, C. E., Dressler, C., Lippman, D. N., Lively, T. J., & White, C. E. (2004). Closing the gap: Addressing the vocabulary needs of English-language learners in bilingual and mainstream classrooms. *Reading Research Quarterly, 39*(20), 188–215.

Chiesi, H., Spilich, G., & Voss, J. (1979). Acquisition of domain-related information in relation to high- and low-domain knowledge. *Journal of Verbal Learning and Verbal Behavior, 18,* 257–274.

Cloud, N. (1993). Language, culture & disability: Implications for instruction and teacher preparation. *Teacher Education and Special Education, 16*(1), 60–72.

Cloud, N. (2006). How can we best serve English language learners who have special needs, such as a disability? In E. Hamayan & R. Freeman (Eds.), *English language learners at school: A guide for administrators* (pp. 208–209). Philadelphia, PA: Caslon Publishing.

Council for Exceptional Children. (2008). New strategies to help students succeed. *CEC Today*. Retrieved December 16, 2008 from http:// www.cec.sped.org/AM/ Template.cfm?Section=Home&TEMPLATE=/CM/ ContentDisplay.cfm&CONTENTID=11474.

Council for Exceptional Children. (2009). Special Issue: Evidence-based practices for reading, math, writing and behavior. *Exceptional Children 75,* 3.

Coxhead, A. (2000). A new academic word list. *TESOL Quarterly, 34*(2), 213–238.

Crossley, S., McCarthy, P., Louwerse, M., & McNamara, D. (2007). A linguistic analysis of simplified and authentic texts. *The Modern Language Journal, 19*(2), 15–30.

Cummins, J. (1984). *Bilingualism and special education: Issues in assessment and pedagogy*. Clevedon, England: Multilingual Matters.

Cummins, J. (2000). *Language, power and pedagogy*. Clevedon, England: Multilingual Matters.

Cunningham, P. (2006). High-poverty schools that beat the odds. *The Reading Teacher, 60*(4) 382–385.

Danielson, C. (2007) *Enhancing professional practice: A framework for teaching* (2nd ed.). Alexandria, VA: Association for Supervision and Curriculum Development.

Darling-Hammond, L. (2000). Teacher quality and student achievement: A review of state policy evidence. *Education Policy Analysis, 8*(1).

Deno, S. L. (1985). Curriculum-based measurement: The emerging alternative. *Exceptional Children, 52*(3), 219–232.

Denton, C. A., Wexler, J., Vaughn, S., & Bryan, D. (2008). Intervention provided to linguistically diverse middle school students with severe reading difficulties. *Learning Disabilities Research & Practice, 23*(2), 79–89.

Diller, D. (2007). *Making the most of small groups: Differentiation for all.* Portland, ME: Stenhouse.

Dole, J., Duffy, G., Roehler, L., & Pearson, P. D. (1991). Moving from the old to the new: Research in reading comprehension instruction. *Review of Educational Research, 61,* 239–264.

Duffy, H. (n.d.). *Meeting the needs of significantly struggling learners in high school: A look at approaches to tiered intervention*. Washington, DC: National High School Center, U.S. Department of Education. Retrieved on January 27, 2010 from 222.rti4success .org.

East, B. (2006). Myths about Response to Intervention (RTI) implementation. Retrieved December 12, 2009 from http:// www.rtinetwork.org/Learn/What/are/MythsAboutRTI.

Echevarria, J. (1995). Interactive reading instruction: A comparison of proximal and distal effects of instructional conversations. *Exceptional Children, 61*(6), 536–552.

Echevarria, J., & Graf, V. (1988). California bilingual special education model sites (1984–1986): Programs and research. In A. Ortiz & B. Ramirez (Eds.), *Schools and the culturally diverse student: Promising practices and future directions* (pp. 104–111). Reston, VA: Council for Exceptional Children.

Echevarria, J., & Graves, A. (2010). *Sheltered content instruction: Teaching English learners with diverse abilities* (4th ed.). Boston, MA: Allyn & Bacon.

Echevarria, J., & Hasbrouck, J. (2009). *Response to intervention and English learners* (CREATE Brief). Washington, DC: Center for Research on the Educational Achievement and Teaching of English Language Learners.

Echevarria, J., Richards, C., Canges, R., & Francis, D. (2009). *Using the SIOP® Model to promote the acquisition of language and science concepts with English learners.* Manuscript submitted for publication.

Echevarria, J., Short, D., & Powers, K. (2006). School reform and standards-based education: An instructional model for English language learners. *Journal of Educational Research, 99*(4), 195–211.

Echevarria, J., Short, D., & Vogt, M.E. (2008). *Implementing the SIOP® Model through effective professional development and coaching*. Boston, MA: Allyn & Bacon.

Echevarria, J., Vogt, M.E., & Short, D. (2008). *Making content comprehensible for English learners: The SIOP® Model* (3rd ed.). Boston, MA: Allyn & Bacon.

Echevarria, J., Vogt, M.E., & Short, D. (2010a). *Making content comprehensible for elementary English learners: The SIOP® Model.* Boston, MA: Allyn & Bacon.

Echevarria, J., Vogt, M.E., & Short, D. (2010b). *Making content comprehensible for secondary English learners: The SIOP® Model.* Boston, MA: Allyn & Bacon.

Echevarria, J., Vogt, M.E., & Short, D. (2010c). *The SIOP® Model for Teaching Mathematics to English Learners.* Boston, MA: Allyn & Bacon.

Ehren, B. J. (n.d.). *Response to Intervention in secondary schools: Is it on your radar screen?* Retrieved on February 5, 2010 from www.rtinetwork.org.

Elbaum, B., Vaughn, S., & Hughes, M. (1999). Grouping practices and reading outcomes for students with disabilities. *Exceptional Children, 65*(3), 399–415.

Engelmann, S., Becker, W. C., Carnine, D. W., & Gersten, R. (1988). The Direct Instruction Follow Through Model: Design and outcomes. *Education & Treatment of Children, 11*(4), 303–317.

Ervin, R. A., Schaughency, E., Goodman, S. D., McGlinchey, M. T., & Matthews, A. (2006). Merging research and practice agendas to address reading and behavior school-wide. *School Psychology Review, 35,* 198–223.

Figueroa, R. (2002). Assessment and identification: Toward a new model of assessment. In A. Artiles & A. Ortiz, (Eds.), *English language learners with special education needs.* Washington, DC: Center for Applied Linguistics.

Figueroa, R. (2007). Assessment and identification. In A. Artiles & A. Ortiz, (Eds.), *English language learners with special education needs.* Washington, DC: Center for Applied Linguistics.

Fuchs, D. (2009). *Determining which students will receive Tier 3 intervention.* Iris Center. Retrieved on December 15, 2009 from http://iris.peabody.vanderbilt.edu/rti05_tier3/rti_tier3_04.html.

Fuchs, D., & Deshler, D. (2007). What we need to know about responsiveness to intervention (and shouldn't be afraid to ask). *Learning Disabilities Research & Practice, 22*(2), 129–136.

Fuchs, L. (2009). How can Tier 3 intervention be implemented? Retrieved on December 10, 2009 from http://iris.peabody.vanderbilt.edu/rti05_tier3/rti_tier3_05.html.

Fuchs, L., & Fuchs, D. (2007). The role of assessment in the three-tier approach to reading instruction. In D. Haager, J. Klinger, & S. Vaughn (Eds.), *Evidence-based reading practices for response to intervention.* Baltimore, MD: Paul H. Brookes Publishing Co.

Fuchs, L. S., Fuchs, D., & Hamlett, C. L. (1993). Formative evaluation of academic progress: How much growth can we expect? *School Psychology Review, 22*(1), 27–48.

Futrell, M. & Gomez, J. (2008). How tracking creates a poverty of learning. *Educational Leadership, 65*(8), 74–78.

Garcia, E., & Hamayan, E. (2006). What is the role of culture in language learning? In E. Hamayan & R. Freeman (Eds.), *English language learners at school: A guide for administrators* (pp. 61–64). Philadelphia, PA: Caslon Publishing.

Garcia, E., & Jensen, B. (2007). Helping young Hispanic learners. *Educational Leadership, 64*(6), 34–39.

Gedney, S. (Ed.). (2009). Structuring language instruction to advance stalled English learners. Aiming High. Santa Rosa, CA: Sonoma County Office of Education (www.scoe.org).

Genesee, F., Lindholm-Leary, K., Saunders, B., & Christian. D. (2006). *Educating English language learners: A synthesis of research evidence.* New York, NY: Cambridge University Press.

Gerber, M., Jimenez, T., Leafstedt, J., Villaruz, J., Richards, C., & English, J. (2004). English reading effects of small-group intensive intervention in Spanish for K–1 English learners. *Learning Disabilities Research and Practice, 19*(4), 239–251.

Gersten, R., Baker, S. K., Shanahan, T., Linan-Thompson, S., Collins, P., & Scarcella, R. (2007). *Effective literacy and English language instruction for ELs in the elementary grades: A practice guide* (NCEE 2007-4011). Washington, DC: National Center for Education Evaluation and Regional Assistance, Institute of Education Sciences, U.S. Department of Education. Retrieved from http://ies.ed.gov/ncee.

Gersten, R., Brengelman, S., & Jiminez, R. (1994). Effective instruction for culturally and linguistically diverse students: A reconceptualization. *Focus on Exceptional Children, 27,* 1–16.

Gersten, R., & Dimino, J. (2006). RTI (Response to Intervention): Rethinking special education for students with reading difficulties (yet again). *Reading Research Quarterly, 41,* 99–108.

Glenn, C., & de Jong, E. (1996). *Educating immigrant children: Schools and language minorities in twelve nations.* New York, NY: Garland Publishing.

Goldenberg, C. (2004). *Successful school change.* New York, NY: Teachers College Press.

Goldenberg, C. (2006). Involving parents of English learners in their children's schooling. *Instructional Leader,* Texas Elementary Principals and Supervisors Association.

Goldenberg, C. (2008). Teaching English language learners: What the research does—and does not—say. *The American Educator, 32*(2), 8–23.

Goldenberg, C., Rueda, R. S., & August, D. (2008). Sociocultural contexts and literacy development. In D. August &

T. Shanahan (Eds.), *Developing reading and writing in second-language learners: Lessons from the Report of the National Literacy Panel on Language-Minority Children and Youth*. New York, NY: Routledge, the Center for Applied Linguistics, and the International Reading Association.

Goldenberg, C., & Saunders, W. (In press). Research to guide English language development instruction. In California Department of Education (Eds.), *Improving education for English learners: Research-based approaches*. Sacramento, CA: CDE Press.

Graves, A. W., Plasencia-Peinado, J., Deno, S., & Johnson, J. (2005). Formatively evaluating the reading progress of first-grade English learners in multiple language classrooms. *Remedial & Special Education, 38,* 245–255.

Gresham, F. M., MacMillan, D. L., Beebe-Frankenberger, M. E., & Bocian, K. M. (2000). Treatment integrity in learning disabilities intervention research: Do we really know how treatments are implemented? *Learning Disabilities Research & Practice, 15*(4), 198–205.

Haager, D., & Mahdavi, J. (2007). Teacher roles in implementing interventions. In D. Haager, J. Klinger, & S. Vaughn (Eds.), *Evidence-based reading practices for Response to Intervention* (pp. 245–264). Baltimore, MD: Paul H. Brookes Publishing.

Hale, J. (2001). *Learning while black: Creating educational excellence for African American children*. Baltimore, MD: Johns Hopkins.

Harry, B., Klinger, J., & Cramer, E. (2007). *Case studies of minority student placement in special education*. New York, NY: Teacher College Press.

Hauerwas, L. B., & Goessling, D. P. (2008). Who are the interventionists? Guidelines for paraeducators in RTI. *Teaching Exceptional Children Plus, 4*(3) Article 4. Retrieved 4/28/10 from http://escholarship.bc.edu/education/tecplus/vol4/iss3/art4

Hiebert, E., Stewart, J., & Uzicanin, M. (2010). *A comparison of word features affecting word recognition of at-risk beginning readers and their peers*. Paper presented at the annual meeting of the Society for the Scientific Study of Reading on July 10, 2010, Berlin.

Honigsfeld, A., & Cohan, A. (2008). The power of two: Lesson study and SIOP® help teachers instruct ELLs. *Journal of Staff Development, 29*(1), p. 24–28.

Honigsfeld, A., & Dove, M. (2010). *Collaboration and co-teaching: Strategies for English learners*. Thousand Oaks, CA: Corwin Press.

Horowitz, S. (2009). *Learning disabilities: What they are, and what they are not*. National Center for Learning Disabilities. Retrieved January 28, 2010 from http://www.ncld.org/ld-basics/ld-explained/basic-facts/learning-disabilities-what-they-are-and-what-they-are-not

Horowitz. S., & Stecker, D. (2007). *Learning disabilities checklist of signs and symptoms*. National Center for Learning Disabilities. Retrieved January 25, 2010 from http://www.ncld.org/publications-a-more/checklists-worksheets-a-forms/ld-checklist-of-signs-and-sympstons.

Hosp, J., & Madyun, N. (2007). Addressing disproportionality with response to intervention. In S. Jimerson, M. Burns, & A. VanDer Heyden (Eds.), *Handbook of Response to Intervention*. New York: Springer.

International Reading Association . (February/March, 2010). Six guiding principles for Response to Intervention, *Reading Today*. Newark, DE, p. 1.

Jensen, E. (2005). *Teaching with the brain in mind* (2nd ed.). Alexandria, VA: Association for Supervision and Curriculum Development.

Jiménez, R. T., Garcia, G. E., & Pearson, P. D. (1996). The reading strategies of bilingual Latina/o students who are successful English readers: Opportunities and obstacles. *Reading Research Quarterly, 57*(6), 576–578.

Johns, J. (2008). *Basic reading inventory: Pre-primer thorough grade twelve and early literacy assessments* (10th ed.). Dubuque, IA: Kendall Hunt.

Kamil, M. L., Borman, G. D., Dole, J., Kral, C. C., Salinger, T., & Torgesen, J. (2008). *Improving adolescent literacy: Effective classroom and intervention practices: A Practice Guide* (NCEE #2008-4027). Washington, DC: National Center for Education Evaluation and Regional Assistance, Institute of Education Sciences, U.S. Department of Education. Retrieved from http://ies.ed.gov/ncee/wwc.

Kelly, P., Gomez-Bellenge, F., Chen, J., & Schultz, M. (2008). Learner outcomes for English language learner low readers in an early intervention. *TESOL Quarterly, 42*(2), 225–260.

Klinger, J., & Edwards, P. (2006). Cultural considerations with Response to Intervention models. *Reading Research Quarterly, 41*(1), 108–117.

Klinger, J., Sorrells, A., & Barrera, M. (2007). Considerations when implementing Response to Intervention with culturally and linguistically diverse students. In D. Haager, J. Klinger, & S. Vaughn (Eds.), *Evidence-based reading practices for response to intervention*. Baltimore, MD: Paul H. Brookes Publishing Co.

Lenz, B. K., Ehren, B. J., & Deshler, D. D. (2005). The content literacy continuum: A school reform framework for improving adolescent literacy for all students. *Teaching Exceptional Children, 37*(6), 60–63.

Lesaux, N., & Giva, E. (2008). Development of literacy in second-language learners. In D. August & T. Shanahan (Eds.), *Developing reading and writing in second-language learners: Lessons from the Report of the National Literacy Panel on Language-Minority Children*

and Youth. New York, NY: Routledge, the Center for Applied Linguistics, and the International Reading Association.

Lyster, R. (2007). *Learning and teaching languages through content: A counterbalanced approach*. Philadelphia, PA: John Benjamin.

Marston, D., Reschly, A., Lau, M., Muyskens, P., & Canter, A. (2007). Historical perspectives and current trends in problem solving. In D. Haager, J. Klinger, & S. Vaughn (Eds.), *Evidence-based reading practices for response to intervention*. Baltimore, MD: Paul H. Brookes Publishing Co.

Marzano, R., Pickering, D., & Pollock, J. (2001). *Classroom instruction that works*. Alexandria, VA: Association for Supervision and Curriculum Development.

McCardle, P., Mele-McCarthy, J., Cutting, L., Leos, L., & D'Emilio, T. (2005). Learning disabilities in English language learners: Identifying the issues. *Learning Disabilities Research & Practice, 20*(1), 1–5.

McIntyre, E., Kyle, D., Munoz, M., Chen, C.-T., & Beldon, S. (In press). Teacher learning and ELL reading achievement in sheltered instruction classrooms: Linking professional development to student development. *Literacy Research and Instruction*.

McMaster, K., Kung, S., Han, I., & Cao, M. (2008). Peer-assisted learning strategies: A tier 1 approach to promoting English learners' response to intervention. *Exceptional Children, 74*(2) 194–214.

Moje, E. B. (1996). "I teach students, not subjects": Teacher-student relationships as contexts for secondary literacy. *Reading Research Quarterly, 31*(2), 172–195.

Moje, E. B. (2008). Foregrounding the disciplines in secondary literacy teaching and learning: A call for change. *Journal of Adolescent & Adult Literacy, 52*(2), 96–107.

Moll, L., Amanti, C., Neff, D., & Gonzalez, N. (1992). Funds of knowledge for teaching: Using a qualitative approach to connect homes and classrooms. *Theory Into Practice. 31*(2), 132–141.

National Assessment of Educational Progress (NAEP). (2008). *The nation's report card*. Retrieved on February 10, 2010 from http://nartionsreportcard.gov

National Center for Education Statistics. (2002). *1999–2000 Schools and staffing survey*. Washington DC: U.S. Department of Education, Office of Educational Research and Improvement.

National Center for Learning Disabilities. (2008). *RTI gets promoted to secondary schools: An interview with Barbara J. Ehren & Kathleen Whitmire*. Retrieved on February 5, 2010 from http://ncldtalks.org.

National Center on Student Progress Monitoring. (2009). *Common questions about progress monitoring*. Retrieved from http:// www.studentprogress.org/progresmon.asp#1 on June 17, 2009.

National Council of Teachers of Mathematics (NCTM). *Principles and standards for school mathematics*. Reston, VA: Retrieved May 14, 2009 at http://www.nctm.org/standards/default. aspx?id=58.

National Reading Panel. (2000). *Teaching children to read: An evidence-based assessment of the scientific research literature on reading and its implications for reading instruction*. Washington, DC: National Institute of Child Health and Human Development, National Institutes of Health.

O'Brien, D. G., Stewart, R. A., & Moje, E. B. (1995). Why content literacy is difficult to infuse into the secondary school: Complexities of curriculum, pedagogy, and school culture. *Reading Research Quarterly, 30*(3), 442–463.

O'Malley, J. J., & Chamot, A. U. (1990). *Learning strategies in second language acquisition*. Cambridge: Cambridge University Press.

Oakes, J. (1985). *Keeping track: How schools structure inequality*. New Haven, CT: Yale University Press.

Oakes, J. (1987). Tracking in secondary schools: A contextual perspective. *Educational Psychologist, 22*(2), 129–153.

Olson, S., Daly, E., Andersen, M., Turner, A., & LeClair, C. (2007). Assessing student response to intervention. In S. Jimerson, M. Burns, & A. Van Der Heyden (Eds.), *Handbook of Response to Intervention*, New York, NY: Springer.

Ortiz, A. (1997). Learning disabilities occurring concomitantly with linguistic differences. *Journal of Learning Disabilities, 30*, 321–332.

Ortiz, A., & Yates, J. (2002). Considerations in the assessment of English language learners referred to special education. In A. Artiles & A. Ortiz, (Eds.), *English language learners with special education needs*. Washington, DC: Center for Applied Linguistics.

Padron, Y., Waxman, H., & Rivera, H. (2002). *Educating Hispanic students: Obstacles and avenues to improved academic achievement*. Santa Cruz, CA: Center for Research on Education, Diversity & Excellence.

Payne, R. (2008). Nine powerful practices. *Educational Leadership, 65*(7), 48–52.

Pennsylvania Department of Education. (2008). *Response to Intervention (RtI). Framework for secondary schools: Guidelines and recommendations*. Pennsylvania Training and Technical Assistance Network. Retrieved on February 5, 2010 from www.pattan.net.

Perie, M., Grigg, W. W., & Donahue, P. L. (2005). *The nation's report card: Reading 2005* (NCES 2006-451). National Center for Educational Statistics, U.S. Department of

Education. Washington, DC: Government Printing Office.

Pitcher, S. M., Albright, L. K., DeLaney, C. J., Walker, N. T., Seunarinesingh, K., & Mogge, S. (2007). Assessing adolescents' motivation to read. *Journal of Adolescent & Adult Literacy, 50*(5), 378–396.

Pressley, M. (2005). *Literacy-instructional effective classrooms and schools… And why I am so worried about comprehension instruction even in places like these!* Keynote address presented to the Research Institute of the 51st International Reading Association Annual Convention, Chicago, IL.

Ramirez, D., Yuen, S., Ramey, D., & Pasta, D. (1991). *Executive summary: Final report: Longitudinal study of structured English immersion strategy, early-exit and late-exit transitional bilingual education programs for language minority children.* Submitted to the U.S. Department of Education. San Mateo, CA: Aguirre International.

Rampey, B. D., Dion, G. S., & Donahue, P. L. (2009). The nation's report card: Trends in academic progress in reading and mathematics 2008. Retrieved on February 9, 2010 from www.nces .ed.gov/nationsreportcard/pubs/main2008/2009479.asp.

Reeves, D. (December 2008/January 2009). Looking deeper into the data. *Educational Leadership, 66*(4), 89–90.

Richards, C., & Leafstedt, J. (2010). *Early reading intervention: Strategies and methods for struggling readers.* Boston, MA: Allyn & Bacon.

Riches, C., & Genesee, F. (2006). Literacy: Crosslinguistic & crossmodal issues. In F. Genesee, K. Lindholm-Leary, W. Saunders, & D. Christian (Eds.), *Educating English language learners: A synthesis of research evidence.* New York, NY: Cambridge University Press.

Ruddell, M. R. (2007). *Teaching content reading and writing* (5th ed.). Hoboken, NJ: Wiley Jossey-Bass Education.

Rueda, R. (1989). Defining mild disabilities with language minority students. *Exceptional Children, 56*(2), 131–128.

Ruiz, N. (1989). An optimal learning environment for Rosemary. *Exceptional Children, 56*(2), 130–144.

Ruiz, N. (1995). The social construction of ability and disability: Profiles types of Latino children identified as language learning disabled. *Journal of Learning Disabilities, 28*, 476–490.

Rumberger, R., Gandara, P., & Merino, B. (2006). Where California's English learners attend school and why it matters. *UC Linguistic Minority Research Institute Newsletter, 15*(2), 1–3.

Salend, S., & Salinas, A. (2003). Language differences or learning difficulties. *Teaching Exceptional Children, 35*(4), 36–43.

Saunders, W. M., Foorman, B. R., & Carlson, C. D. (November, 2006). Do we need a separate block of time for oral English language development in programs for English learners? *Elementary School Journal, 107*(2), 181–198.

Saunders, W. M., Goldenberg, C. N., & Gallimore, R. (2009). Increasing achievement by focusing grade level teams on improving classroom learning: A prospective, quasi-experimental study of Title I schools. *American Educational Research Journal, 46*(4), 1006–1033.

Scammacca, N., Roberts, G., Vaughn. S., Edmonds, M., Wexler, J., Reutebuch, C. K., & Torgesen, J. K. (2007), Interventions for adolescent struggling readers: A meta-analysis with implications for practice. Portsmouth, NH: RMC Research Corporation, Center on Instruction.

Scarcella, R. (2003). *Academic English: A conceptual framework* (Technical report 2003-1). Santa Barbara, CA: Linguistic Minority Research Institute.

Schmoker, M. (2007). Reading, writing and thinking for all. *Educational Leadership*, 64(7) 63–66.

Shannon, B. S., & Bylsma, P. (2007). *Nine characteristics of high performing schools.* Olympia, WA: Office of Superintendent of Public Instruction. Available online at http://www.k12.wa.us/research/default.aspx

Shearer, B. A., Ruddell, M. R., & Vogt, M.E. (2001). Successful middle school intervention: Negotiated strategies and individual choice. In T. Shanahan & F. V. Rodriguez (Eds.), *National Reading Conference Yearbook, 50* (pp. 558–571), National Reading Conference.

Short, D. (2002). Language learning in sheltered social studies classes. *TESOL Journal, 11*(1), 18–24.

Short, D., Fidelman, C., & Louguit, M. (2010). *Developing academic language in English learners through sheltered instruction.* Manuscript submitted for publication.

Short, D., & Fitzsimmons, S. (2006). *Double the work: Challenges and solutions to acquiring language and academic literacy for adolescent English language learners.* A Report to the Carnegie Corporation. New York, NY: Alliance for Education.

Short, D., Vogt, M.E., & Echevarria, J. (2010a). *The SIOP® Model for teaching science to English learners.* Boston, MA: Allyn & Bacon.

Short, D., Vogt, M.E., & Echevarria, J. (2010b). *The SIOP® Model for teaching history-social studies to English learners.* Boston, MA: Allyn & Bacon.

Smith, D. D., & Tyler, N. C. (2010). *Introduction to special education: Making a difference* (7th ed.). Columbus, OH: Pearson/Merrill.

Sobel, A., & Kugler, E. (2007). Building partnerships with immigrant parents. *Educational Children, 2,* 121–128.

Sox, A., & Rubinstein-Ávila, E. (2009). WebQuests for English-language learners: Essential elements for design. *Journal of Adolescent & Adult Literacy, 53*(1), 38–48.

Sturtevant, E. G., Boyd, F. B., Brozo, W. G., Hinchman, K. A., Moore, D. W., & Alvermann, D. E. (2006). *Principled practices for adolescent literacy. A framework for instruction and policy.* Mahwah, NJ: Erlbaum.

Sturtevant, E. G., & Kim, G. S. (2010). Literacy motivation and school/non-school literacies among students enrolled in a middle-school ESOL program. *Literacy Research and Instruction, 49*(1), 68–85.

Suarez-Orozco, C., Suarez-Orozco, M., & Todorova, I. (2008). *Learning a new land: Immigrant students in American society.* Cambridge, MA: Harvard University Press.

Tatum, A. (2008). Toward a more anatomically complete model of literacy instruction: A focus on African American male adolescents and texts. *Harvard Educational Review, 78*(1), 155–182.

Thompson, G. (2004). *Through ebony eyes: What teachers need to know but are afraid to ask about African American students.* San Francisco, CA: Jossey-Bass.

Thompson, G. (2008). Beneath the apathy. *Educational Leadership 65*(6), 50–54.

Tomlinson, C. A. (1999). *The differentiated classroom: Responding to the needs of all learners.* Alexandria, VA: ASCD.

Torgesen, J. K. (2000). Individual differences in response to early interventions in reading: The lingering problem of treatment resisters. *Learning Disabilities Research & Practice, 15*, 55–64.

Trent, S. C. & Artiles, A. (2007). Today's multicultural, bilingual, and diverse schools. In R. Turnbull, A. Turnbull, M. Shank, & S. J. Smith (Eds.), *Exceptional lives: Special education in today's schools.* (5th ed., pp. 56–79). Upper Saddle River, NJ: Pearson.

Trent, S. C., Kea, C., & Oh, K. (2008). Preparing preservice educators for cultural diversity: How far have we come? *Exceptional Children, 74*(3), 328–350.

Tucker, J., & Sornson, R. (2007). One student at a time; one teacher at a time: Reflections on the use of instructional support. In S. Jimerson, M. Burns, & A. VanDer Heyden (Eds.), *Handbook of Response to Intervention* (pp. 269–278). New York, NY: Springer.

Valdes, G. (2001). *Learning and not learning English: Latino students in American schools.* New York, NY: Teachers College Press.

Vanderwood, M., & Nam, J. (2007). Response to intervention for English language learners: Current development and future directions. In S. Jimerson, M. Burns, & A. Van Der Heyden (Eds.), *Handbook of Response to Intervention* (pp. 408–417). New York, NY: Springer.

Vanderwood, M. L., Kinklater, D., & Healy, K. (2008). Predictive accuracy of nonsense word fluency for English language learners. *School Psychology Review, 37*, 5–17.

Vaughn, S., Gersten, R., & Chard, D. (2000). The underlying message in LD intervention research: Findings from research syntheses. *Exceptional Children, 67*, 99–114.

Vaughn, S., & Klinger, J. (2007). Overview of the three-tier model of reading intervention. In D. Haager, J. Klinger, & S. Vaughn (Eds.), Evidence-based reading practices for response to intervention (pp. 3–10). Baltimore, MD: Paul H. Brookes Publishing Co.

Vaughn, S., Linan-Thompson, S., Mathes, P. G., Cirino, P. T., Carlson, C. D., Pollard-Durodola, S. D., et al. (2006). Effectiveness of Spanish intervention for first grade English language learners at risk for reading difficulties. *Journal of Learning Disabilities, 39*, 56–73.

Vaughn, S., Wanzek, J., Woodruff, A., & Linan-Thompson, S. (2007). Prevention and early identification of students with reading disabilities. In D. Haager, J. Klingner, & S. Vaughn (Eds.), *Evidence-based reading practices for Response to Intervention* (pp. 11–27). Baltimore, MD: Paul H. Brookes.

Vellutino, F., Scanlon, D., & Zhang, H. (2007) Identifying reading disability based on response to intervention: Evidence from early intervention research. In S. Jimerson, M. Burns & A. VanDer Heyden (Eds.), *Handbook of Response to Intervention.* New York, NY: Springer.

Villegas, A. M., & Lucas, T. (2007). The culturally responsive teacher. *Educational Leadership, 64*(6), 28–33.

Vogt, M.E. (1989). *A study of the congruence between preservice teachers' and cooperating teachers' attitudes and practices toward high and low achievers.* Unpublished doctoral dissertation submitted to the University of California, Berkeley.

Vogt, M.E. (2009). Teachers of English learners: Issues of preparation and professional development. In F. Falk-Ross, S. Szabo, M. B. Sampson, & M. M. Foote (Eds.), *Literacy issues during changing times: A call to action.* Texas A & M University, Commerce: College Reading Association Yearbook, 30, pp. 22–36.

Vogt, M.E., & Echevarria, J. (2008). *99 ideas and activities for teaching English learners with the SIOP® Model.* Boston, MA: Allyn & Bacon.

Vogt, M.E., Echevarria, J., & Short, D. (2010). *The SIOP® Model for Teaching English-Language Arts to English Learners.* Boston, MA: Allyn & Bacon.

Vogt, M.E., & Shearer, B. A. (2011). *Reading specialists and literacy coaches in the real world* (3rd ed.). Boston, MA: Allyn & Bacon.

Wallace, T., Espin, C. A., McMaster, K., Deno, S. L., & Foegen, A. (2007). CBM progress monitoring within a

standards-based system. *The Journal of Special Education, 41*(2), 66–67.

Waxman, H., Gray, J., & Padron, Y. (2003). *Review of research on educational resilience.* Santa Cruz, CA: Center for Research on Education, Diversity & Excellence.

Wayman, M. M., Wallace, T., & Wiley, H. I. (2007). Literature synthesis on curriculum-based measurement in reading. *The Journal of Special Education, 41*(2), 85–120.

Weinstein, R. S. (1985). Student mediation of classroom expectancy effects. In J. Dusek (Ed.), *Teacher expectancies.* Hillsdale, NJ: Lawrence Erlbaum Associates.

Wexler, J., Vaughn, S., Roberts, G., & Denton, C. A. (2010). The efficacy of repeated reading and wide reading practice for high school students with severe reading disabilities. *Learning Disabilities Research & Practice, 25*(1), 2–10.

Zirkel, P. A., & Krohn, N. (2008). RtI after IDEA: A survey of state law. *Teaching Exceptional Children, 40*(3), 71–73.

Zwiers, J. (2008). *Building academic language: Essential practices for content classrooms.* San Francisco, CA: Jossey-Bass; Newark, DE: International Reading Association.